Who Is Jesus?

Who Is
Jesus?

Greg Gilbert

■■ **CROSSWAY**®

WHEATON, ILLINOIS

Who Is Jesus?

Copyright © 2015 by Gregory D. Gilbert

Published by Crossway
               1300 Crescent Street
               Wheaton, Illinois 60187

Cover design: Matthew Wahl

First printing 2015

Printed in the United States of America

Scripture quotations are from the ESV® Bible (The Holy Bible, English Standard Version®), copyright © 2001 by Crossway, a publishing ministry of Good News Publishers. 2011 Text Edition. Used by permission. All rights reserved.

All emphases in Scripture quotations have been added by the author.

Trade paperback ISBN: 978-1-4335-4350-0
ePub ISBN: 978-1-4335-4353-1
PDF ISBN: 978-1-4335-4351-7
Mobipocket ISBN: 978-1-4335-4352-4

Library of Congress Cataloging-in-Publication Data

Gilbert, Greg, 1977–
   Who is Jesus? / Greg Gilbert.
      pages cm. — (9Marks books)
   Includes bibliographical references.
   ISBN 978-1-4335-4350-0 (tp)
   1. Jesus Christ—Person and offices. I. Title.
BT203.G55   2015
232—dc23   2014016639

Crossway is a publishing ministry of Good News Publishers.

LB		27	26	25	24	23	22	21	20	19	18	17
16	15	14	13	12	11	10	9	8	7	6	5	4

To Justin, Jack, and Juliet

Contents

Foreword

Have you ever mistaken a person for someone else? I remember being at a party with my best friend in high school. We had just arrived when we saw our friend Nicole standing in the corner having a good time. We had spent time with Nicole and her pregnant friend the day before, so we decided to walk over and greet them. My best friend said hey to Nicole, rubbed her friend's belly with a kind smile, and thoughtfully asked, "How's the baby?" The only problem was that this was a different friend. And she wasn't in the least bit pregnant. Man, was I glad I didn't speak up first.

It can be embarrassing and humorous to make mistakes about other people's identities. You risk looking dumb and offending others, so it's best to be sure before you speak up.

The book you hold in your hands is about recognizing someone else's identity, but the stakes are much higher. When we talk about Jesus, we're in a totally different category than recognizing old friends or acquaintances. When we're mistaken about Jesus's identity, it's more than embarrassing—it's tragic.

This is why Greg Gilbert states from the outset that the title of this book, *Who Is Jesus?*, is the most important question we'll ever ask. That may sound ridiculous to seekers, skeptics, and maybe even some Christians, but if you keep reading, you will see why it's such a vital question. Sure, we're not going to run into the Prince of Peace on the street or at a party, so it's not about putting a name with a face. It's about responding to him with the honor and trust that he deserves.

For example, Greg writes, "Once you begin to understand that Jesus is in fact God, and that he is in a unique and exclusive relationship with God the Father, you also begin to understand that if you want to know the God who created you, then you need to know Jesus. There's just no other way."

If Jesus was just another guy, then knowing him makes no difference. But if Jesus is the Son of God and the only Savior of the world, then knowing him makes all the difference.

Too often we've mistaken Jesus for just another man. Or just another good teacher. Or just another prophet. But none of those descriptions is enough. So in this important little book, Greg helps us to think rightly about who Jesus actually is.

I love *Who Is Jesus?* because it's engaging. I actually enjoyed reading it. It's simple enough for anybody to read, and it addresses real questions. I also love this book because it's filled with Scripture. Greg isn't trying to conjure up new ways to look at Jesus. He's interested only in the actual historical truth. Who is this Jesus and why does he matter? Rather than listen to historians who never saw him, Greg focuses on the testimony of reliable eyewitnesses who met him. He focuses on God's Word. This makes for an authoritative, potentially life-changing book.

Jesus made some radical claims, and he's the most talked about person in all of history. Who did he claim to be? And is that who he really is? I can think of no better small book to help you answer those questions. I think you'll be as blessed by it as I was.

Trip Lee
Rapper; Pastor; author,
*Rise: Get Up and Live in
God's Great Glory*

1

What Do You Think?

Who do you think Jesus is?

Maybe you've never really given it much thought. In a way, that's entirely understandable. After all, we're talking about a man who was born in the first century into an obscure Jewish carpenter's family. He never held any political office, never ruled any nation, never commanded any armies. He never even met a Roman emperor. Instead, for three-and-a-half years this man Jesus simply taught people about ethics and spirituality, he read and explained the Jewish Scriptures to Jewish people, and if the eyewitness accounts of his life are to be believed at all, he also did some pretty out-of-the-ordinary things. But then again, Jesus also ran bitterly afoul of the authorities of his day, and not long after he started his public ministry, he wound up being executed on a cross by one of Rome's many provincial governors—a kind of imperial middle manager for the people who had the real power.

On top of that, all this happened some two thousand years

ago. So why are we still talking about him? Why is this man Jesus so . . . inescapable?

Give Jesus a Chance

Regardless of what you personally think about him, surely we can agree that Jesus is a towering figure in the history of the world. One respected historian put Jesus's influence like this: "If it were possible, with some sort of super-magnet, to pull up out of that history every scrap of metal bearing at least a trace of his name, how much would be left?"[1] That's a good question, and the answer is probably, "Not much!"

But it's not just that Jesus is inescapable in some distant, historical kind of way. He's also inescapable in a much closer way than that. Think about it: You probably have at least one or two acquaintances who would say that they are Christians. Maybe they even go to church regularly and sing songs about— or even *to*—Jesus. If you press them on it, they might even say that they have a *relationship* with him, and that their lives in one way or another are organized around him. Not only that, but your city is likely dotted with church buildings of various kinds. Some of those buildings probably have thriving communities of Christians who gather in them on Sundays. Others probably aren't even churches at all anymore. But the point is that everywhere you look, if you're paying attention, you'll see reminders of this one particular man who lived about two millennia ago. And all of it presses the question on us: who is he?

---

[1] Jaroslav Pelikan, *Jesus through the Centuries: His Place in the History of Culture* (Yale University Press, 1999), 1.

It's not an easy question to answer, mainly because we haven't managed to come to any society-wide consensus about who Jesus really was . . . or is. True, very few people doubt his existence anymore. The basic facts of his life—where and when he lived, how he died—are all pretty well agreed upon. But there's still massive disagreement, even among people who call themselves Christians, about the *significance* of his life and death. Was he a prophet? A teacher? Something entirely different? Was he the Son of God, or just an unusually gifted man? And for that matter, who did *he* think he was? His death at the hands of the Romans—was that part of the plan all along, or did he just get caught in the wrong place at the wrong time? And then there's the biggest question of all: After he was executed, did Jesus stay dead like the rest of us do, or did he . . . not?

For all the disagreement, though, everyone seems to agree on one thing: Jesus was an extraordinary person. He did things and said things that ordinary people simply don't do and say. Even more, the things Jesus said weren't just witty proverbs or ethical gems. They weren't pieces of advice on how to live better in the world. No, Jesus said things like, "I and the Father [by which he meant God] are one," and, "If you have seen me, you have seen the Father." And, maybe most shocking of all, "No one comes to the Father except through me."[2]

You see what I mean? Ordinary people don't say those sorts of things! God and I are one? No one comes to God except by me? Those aren't ethical teachings that you can decide to

---

[2] John 10:30; 14:6

incorporate into your life or not. They are *claims*. They are Jesus saying what he thinks is the *truth*.

Now of course you may not accept what he says. You may reject it outright. But think about it: Wouldn't it make sense not to do that too quickly? Wouldn't it make sense to get to know this man a bit before you completely toss off what he says about you? Let me be bold and make a request, since you've been so kind as to pick up this book and start reading it: Give Jesus a chance. It may be that as you learn more about him, you'll realize that there are actually some very good reasons for believing what he said—about himself, about God, and about *you*.

Where Do You Go to Learn about Jesus?

So . . . how do you get to know a guy who lived two thousand years ago? Even if you start with a belief in the resurrection, it's not like we can knock on the door of heaven and sit down with Jesus over a cup of coffee. So where do you go to learn about Jesus? Many historical documents make reference to the existence, life, death, and even resurrection of Jesus, and you might be able to pick up a thing or two about him there. But most of those documents have at least a couple of problems. For one thing, many of them were written so late—sometimes hundreds of years after Jesus—that they really don't help us much in knowing who he *really* was. Not only that, but in most cases even the best of those documents just don't say much about him. They're concerned with other issues, and so they only mention Jesus or allude to him rather than tell us about him in any detail.

There is, however, one massive treasure trove of information about Jesus—detailed, personal, eyewitness, blow-by-blow accounts of what he said, what he did, and who he was. That's the Bible.

Now wait a second before you close this book! I know some people recoil when the Bible is mentioned because they think of it as "the Christians' book," and therefore they think it's biased and useless for getting accurate information. If that's what you think, then believe it or not, I'd say you're half right. The Bible *is* in fact the Christians' book. Without doubt, the New Testament documents that make up the second part of the Bible were written by people who believed what Jesus said, and they also believed that the Old Testament documents looked forward to his coming. They were believers. That much is undeniable. But that *doesn't* mean that those people had some insidious agenda. Think about it: What could their agenda possibly have been? To make a name for themselves? To make money? To become powerful rulers of a very rich church? You can speculate about that, of course, but if that's what they were aiming for, then the plan failed spectacularly. Most of the people who wrote the New Testament documents knew they could be killed for what they said about Jesus. *And yet they kept saying it.*

Do you see the point? If your goal in writing an account of something is just to get noticed, to become powerful, or to wind up rich, then you don't stick to the story once the jig is up and your head is about to come off. The only way you stick by the story under those circumstances is if your goal is to *tell what really happened.* That's what we have in the Bible—a collection of eyewitness accounts by people who believed what Jesus said, and who wrote their books in order to give an accurate description of who he was, what he said, and what he did. So how do you get to know Jesus? The best way is by reading those documents—that is, by reading the Bible.

Now, Christians believe that the Bible is way more than just a collection of the best information about Jesus we can get. They believe it is the Word of God, meaning that God himself led the men who wrote it to write what he himself wanted to say, so that everything they wrote was absolutely true. You've probably already guessed this, but I am a Christian myself, and I believe that about the Bible.

But maybe that's a bridge too far for you right now. That's OK. Even if you don't believe that the Bible is the Word of God, the documents it contains are still a matter of history. They're still the writings of people who intended to give an accurate account of Jesus. So if nothing else, approach them like that for now. Ask questions of them, read them critically and carefully just like you would any other historical document. Ask yourself, "Do I think this is true, or do I not?" All I'm asking is that you approach these documents fairly. Don't just drop them with a thud into some box labeled "Religious Junk" and decide from the outset that they must be silly, primitive, and false.

Look, the people who wrote the documents in the New Testament were smart people. They were residents and even citizens of the most powerful empire on the face of the planet.

They read philosophy and literature that we still read in our schools today. (In fact, if you're anything like me, they probably read those books more carefully and thoughtfully than you ever did!) What's more, they knew the difference between fact and fiction. They knew what delusion and deceit were, and they understood how those things differed from history and truth. In fact, the New Testament writers maintained the distinctions between such things far more sharply and carefully than we typically do. And what you realize as you read their writings is that they believed what they were saying about this man Jesus. They were *astonished* by it, but they believed it, and they wanted others to believe it, too. So they wrote in the hope that people would read what they said, get to know Jesus as they knew him, and perhaps come to realize that he is in fact worthy to be believed and trusted.

That's what I'm hoping this little book will help you to do—get to know Jesus through the writings of those earliest Christians. We're not going to work page by page through any one of the New Testament documents. Instead, we're going to use all those sources to try to get to know Jesus in the same way that one who was following him might have experienced him—first as an extraordinary man who did wholly unexpected things, but then with the quickly dawning realization that "extraordinary" doesn't even begin to describe him. Here was a man who claimed to be a prophet, a savior, a king, even God himself—a man whose listeners would have been perfectly justified in chalking him up as a lunatic or a charlatan if only he hadn't kept on *doing* things to back those claims up! Then there was the way he treated people in such unexpected ways—compassion to outcasts, wrath to the powerful, and love toward the unlovable. On top of it all, despite his claims, Jesus didn't act like a king or a god. When he was offered a crown, he refused it, told his followers to keep quiet about who he really was, and talked instead about how the authorities would soon crucify him like a common criminal. But then again, he spoke as if all that were somehow part of his plan all along. Little by little, as they watched him and heard him, Jesus's followers came to believe that he was more than just an extraordinary man. He was more than a teacher, more than a prophet, more than a revolutionary, even more than a king. As one of them put it to him one night, "You are the Christ, the Son of the Living God."[3]

The Most Important Question You'll Ever Consider

So, who is Jesus? That's always been the question. From the moment the shepherds showed up claiming that angels had told them about his birth, to the day he astonished the disciples by calming the sea, to the moment the sun itself stopped shining on the day that he died, everyone was always left asking, "Who is this man?"

Maybe you've come to this book not knowing much about Jesus at all. Maybe you already know quite a bit about Jesus. Either way, I hope that as you read and as we explore his life together, you'll begin to get to know Jesus better—not so much as an academic subject or a religious figure, but as the man

---

[3] Matt. 16:16

the earliest Christians knew personally and as a friend. I hope you'll see what amazed them about him, and I hope you'll come away understanding better why millions say, "That is the man I'm trusting with my eternity."

Beyond that, I also hope that this book will challenge you to take Jesus's claims seriously. When someone claims to be your God, you really only have two choices, right? You can reject the claim or you can accept it. What you *can't* do, at least for very long, is suspend judgment and just see how it plays out. Jesus claimed some amazing things about himself, and also about you. Like it or not, that has radical implications for your life. So I hope this book will challenge you to think hard about Jesus, help you to see those claims and implications more clearly, and lead you to a firm answer to the question, who is Jesus?

Really, it's the most important question you'll ever consider.

2

An Extraordinary Man, and Then Some

It was ten minutes until eight o'clock on a Friday morning when an ordinary-looking man rode up the escalator in a busy Washington, DC, subway station, positioned himself against a wall, and opened his violin case. He pulled out his instrument, its age showing, the finish on its back worn down in some places all the way to the bare wood, and he turned the case around to receive any donations a passer-by might want to give. Then he began to play.

For the next forty-five minutes, as the man played a selection of classical music, over a thousand busy Washingtonians hurried by. One or two cocked their heads, clearly enjoying the sound, but no crowd ever formed around him. One fellow realized he was running three minutes early for work, so he leaned up against a column and listened—for exactly three minutes. Mostly, though, people simply went about their business, reading their papers, listening to their iPods, hurrying away to whatever appointment was showing up next on their screens.

Oh, the music was good. It filled up the arcade, dancing and flowing with incredible precision, and left a few people thinking later that, at least for the split second they'd paid attention, it really did sound like something special. The musician himself didn't look like much—black long-sleeved T-shirt, black pants, Washington Nationals baseball cap—but even so, if you stopped to listen, you couldn't help noticing that this was something more than just another musician playing the violin for pocket change. As a musician, this guy was pretty amazing. One man even commented later that "most people, they play music; they don't *feel* it. Well, that man was *feeling* it. That man was moving. Moving into the sound." If you just listened, he said, "you could tell in one second that this guy was good."[1]

Well, of course you could. Because it wasn't just *any* musician playing the violin that Friday morning in the subway station. It wasn't even a musician who was merely extraordinary. It was Joshua Bell, a thirty-nine-year-old internationally acclaimed virtuoso who normally plays in the most celebrated venues in the world, to crowds who respect him so much that they even stifle their coughs until intermission. Not only that, but that morning Bell was playing some of the most exquisite baroque music ever written, and he was doing it on a three-hundred-year old Stradivarius violin worth an estimated 3.5 million dollars!

The whole scene was calculated to be beautiful: the most beautiful music ever written, played on one of the most finely

---

[1] Gene Weingarten, "Pearls Before Breakfast," *The Washington Post*, April 2007.

calibrated instruments ever crafted, by one of the most talented musicians alive. And yet for all that, you still had to *stop and pay attention* to see just how beautiful it really was.

More Than Extraordinary

So much of life is like that, isn't it? In all the hustle and bustle of work, family, friends, bills, and fun, things like beauty and grandeur sometimes get squeezed out of our minds. We don't have time to appreciate them, because doing so would require us to stop and pay attention to something besides The Urgent.

The same thing is true when it comes to Jesus. Most of us, if we're familiar with him at all, really know him only on the surface. Maybe we know a few of the most famous stories about him, or we can quote some of his more famous sayings. Without a doubt, in his day there was something about Jesus that caught people's attention. He was an extraordinary man. But if you're really going to know Jesus—understand him and grasp his real significance—you have to look a little harder. You have to get beyond the usual debates, the common sound bites, and the familiar stories to see what lies just beyond the surface. Because like the violinist in the subway, it would be a tragic mistake to dismiss Jesus as *merely* an extraordinary man.

So let's be honest. Even if you're not a "religious" kind of person, even if you don't immediately buy into the idea that Jesus was the Son of God or the Savior of the world, you have to admit that he was pretty attention-grabbing. Over and over he did things that caught the eye of his contemporaries, said things that left them amazed at his wisdom, and even confronted them in ways that left them fumbling around for a way to make sense of it all.

At first glance, it would have been easy to mistake Jesus for just one more of the hundreds of religious teachers that debuted, rose, fell, and disappeared in and around first-century Jerusalem. Religious teaching in those days wasn't what it is today. Yes, people listened in order to gain insight, to understand the Scriptures better, and to learn how to live more righteously, but believe it or not, they also listened to religious teaching for sheer entertainment value. After all, if you don't have movies, televisions, and smartphones, what in the world do you do for fun? You pack a picnic and go listen to a preacher!

Strange as that might sound to us, it also helps us understand how unusually *good* Jesus was as a teacher. Because the people of first-century Israel heard so many teachers, and so often, they had opinions about them that were as finely tuned as ours are about movie actors. To put it mildly, they weren't easily impressed. So it's worth stopping to notice what's really going on when the Bible says over and over again that people were "astonished" by Jesus's teaching.

That incredible statement shows up in the Gospels—the Bible's four accounts of Jesus's life—no fewer than ten times.[2] Here's one example, recorded by Matthew after Jesus taught on the side of a mountain: "When Jesus finished these

---

[2] Matt. 7:28; 13:54; 19:25; 22:33; Mark 1:22; 6:2; 7:37; 10:26; 11:18; Luke 4:32

sayings, the crowds were astonished at his teaching, for he was teaching them as one who had authority, and not as their scribes."[3] Don't miss the dig here! The people were saying that the scribes—the ones whose job it was to teach with authority—couldn't hold a candle to Jesus and his teaching. And it was like that everywhere he went and every time he taught.

Sometimes the emotion was described in different words. Look at the reaction the very first time he preached in his hometown: "All spoke well of him and marveled at the gracious words that were coming from his mouth."[4]

And this is how it was in a little fishing village called Capernaum: "They were astonished at his teaching, for he taught them as one who had authority."[5]

Back in his hometown again: "Many who heard him were astonished, saying, 'Where did this man get these things? What is the wisdom given to him?'"[6]

And then at the big show—in Jerusalem at the temple: "The chief priests and the scribes heard it and . . . they feared him, because all the crowd was astonished at his teaching."[7]

Over and over again, the reaction to Jesus was a kind of bewildered, head-shaking incredulity.[8] In a culture that saw teaching as one of its primary forms of public entertainment, Jesus got extraordinary reviews!

---

[3] Matt. 7:28–29
[4] Luke 4:22
[5] Mark 1:22
[6] Mark 6:2
[7] Mark 11:18
[8] See also Matt. 13:54; 22:22, 33

Why So Astonishing?

But why? What was so unusual and so attention-grabbing about Jesus's teaching? Part of it was that once people began to challenge him and ask him questions, Jesus proved to be a masterful chess player. He simply refused to get caught in verbal or intellectual traps, and in fact always managed to turn the heat back on the one who posed the challenge in the first place. And even then, he did it in a way that would not only win the argument, but also spiritually challenge everyone listening. Let me show you an example.

Matthew 22 recounts a time when Jesus was teaching in the temple in Jerusalem and a group of Jewish leaders approached him in order to challenge him. Now, this wasn't an accidental meeting. These leaders had planned the whole thing; the story even starts by saying that the Pharisees "plotted how to entangle him in his words." They also wanted to do it publicly, so they walked up while Jesus was teaching in the temple, probably pushed through a crowd, and interrupted him.

They started with flattery. "Teacher," they crooned, "we know that you are true and teach the way of God truthfully, and you do not care about anyone's opinion, for you are not swayed by appearances." You can see what they're doing here—trying to force Jesus to answer by implying that if he doesn't, he's a charlatan and a quack.

So, the stage set, they ask him a question. "Tell us, then, what you think. Is it lawful to pay taxes to Caesar or not?"[9] Now, that question must have taken some time and planning

---

[9] Matt. 22:15–17

to develop, because it is exquisite in its precision. It's meant to skewer Jesus and, one way or the other, end his influence and perhaps even get him arrested. Here's how: In those days, the prevailing opinion among the Pharisees—and they taught this to the people, too—was that it was actually *sinful* to give any honor at all, including taxes, to a foreign government. To do so, they thought, was inherently to dishonor God himself. So think about it: how did the Pharisees *want* Jesus to answer their question? By publicly agreeing with them that paying the taxes was unlawful and inherently dishonoring to God—or not?

The truth is that they didn't care how he answered. Either way, they thought they had him. On the one hand, if Jesus said, "Yes, it is lawful to pay taxes," the crowd would be furious, and Jesus's influence would be shattered. But on the other hand, if he said, "No, don't pay the taxes," then he was risking the wrath of the Romans for publicly inciting sedition, and he'd probably be arrested—in which case his influence would also be over. Either way, *that's* what the Pharisees wanted—the end of Jesus as a cultural force. But Jesus eluded the trap, turned the whole question on its head, and left them all, again, astonished.

"Show me the coin for the tax," he said. So they handed him one. Jesus looked at it and held it up to the crowd. "Whose likeness and inscription is this?" he asked. It was an easy question. "Caesar's," they answered. And they were correct. Right there on the coin was the face and name of Emperor Tiberius Caesar. That's whose coin it was. It belonged to him. It had his face on it, it was made in his mints, and the Jewish people obviously were happy to use those coins for their own benefit. Given all that, why *shouldn't* they give back to Caesar what was so obviously his? So Jesus said to them, "Therefore render to Caesar the things that are Caesar's, and to God the things that are God's."[10]

Now that seems like a pretty straightforward answer, doesn't it? *It's Caesar's coin; pay the tax*. And yet the Bible says that when the people heard it, they marveled. Why? Well for one thing, Jesus had just redefined the way the Jewish people should think about their relationship to the Romans, and he had undercut the teaching of the Pharisees at the same time. However you sliced it, it simply was not dishonoring to God in any way to give Caesar what was rightfully and obviously his.

But there was another level of depth to what Jesus said, too, and that's what left the people slack-jawed in amazement. Think back to the question Jesus asked when he showed the crowd the coin. "Whose image is on this?" he said, and when they answered that it was Caesar's, Jesus took that as proof of ownership. It was Caesar's image on the coin, and therefore he owned it, and therefore you should give to Caesar what is Caesar's. But—and here's the kicker—you should also render to God what is God's. That is, you should give to God that which has *his* image on it. And what, exactly, is that?

Everyone in the crowd, of course, knew immediately. Jesus was talking about Genesis 1:26, where God announced his plans to create humankind by saying, "Let us make man in our image, after our likeness. . . . So God created man in his

---

[10] Matt. 22:19–21

own image; in the image of God he created him." You see? Jesus was speaking to the people about something much more profound than political philosophy. He was saying that just as Caesar's image is on the coin, so *God's* image is reflected in the very core of your being. And therefore you belong to him! Yes, there's a certain honor that's rendered to Caesar when you acknowledge his image and give his coin back to him. But the infinitely greater honor is rendered when you recognize God's image in yourself and give *yourself*—your heart, soul, mind, and strength—to him.

I hope you can see what Jesus was telling his audience. Far more important than any discussion about political philosophy or one nation's relationship to another is the question of every human being's relationship to God. Jesus was teaching that all of us are made by God, that indeed *you* are made by God. *You* are created in his image and in his likeness, and therefore you belong to him and are accountable to him. And therefore, Jesus said, you should render unto God what is rightfully God's—nothing less than your whole self.

Nobody Did Things Like That

It's no wonder the people were amazed at Jesus's teaching. In just a few sentences he had managed to pull the rug out from under his challengers, redefine the prevailing political theology of his day, and at the same time drill down to the most fundamental fact of human existence. That kind of teaching would have been enough to draw a crowd all by itself!

But then there were the miracles, too. Hundreds and

hundreds of people saw with their own eyes Jesus do things that no human being should be able to do. He healed people of sickness; he made water instantly turn into fine-tasting wine; he told lame people to walk again, and they did; he brought sanity to people who were given over as hopelessly insane. He even made people who were dead come back to life.

It's not that people in those days were just inexcusably gullible about such things. Yes, they lived a long time ago, but that doesn't mean they were primitive or stupid. They didn't walk around claiming to see miracles every day. In fact, that's why every time you read another paragraph of the Bible, you see someone else standing wide-eyed in astonishment at what's just happened. These people were *surprised* to see Jesus doing these things! Even more to the point, precisely because so many people were trying to make a name for themselves as religious gurus, the first-century Jews had gotten incredibly good at identifying charlatans and fakes. They were masters at seeing through magicians' illusions and shaking their heads in laughter as they walked away from yet another guy trying pass off one more parlor trick as a "miracle." The last thing you would call these people was gullible.

But Jesus left them amazed. Unlike all the others, this man really was extraordinary. The other guys pulled rabbits out of hats. This man healed people by the hundreds, even until he was physically worn out and had to sleep. He took two fish and five loaves of bread and made a meal for five thousand people, who quickly became five thousand eyewitnesses to the event. He stopped beside a man who had been lame for years and told him to get up and walk—and the man did. He stood on the prow of a boat and told the ocean to be quiet—and it did. He stood in front of the tomb of a man who had been dead for four days and called to him to come back to life. And the man heard him, stood up, and walked out of the tomb.[11]

Nobody did things like that.

Ever.

And the people were amazed.

All for a Purpose

But even then, there was more. If you really paid attention, if you got beyond the wonder of it all and began to ask the deeper question of *why* was Jesus doing all this, you could begin to see that it was all for a purpose.

You see, with every one of his miracles and in every one of his sermons Jesus was making *and backing up* claims about himself that no human being had ever made before. Take for example Jesus's most famous sermon, the Sermon on the Mount in Matthew 5–7. At first glance, it almost looks like a run-of-the-mill, moralistic, live-like-this-not-like-that harangue. Don't make oaths; don't commit adultery; don't lust; don't get angry. But look again, and you'll realize that "how to behave" is not its main point at all. Actually, the Sermon on the Mount is primarily about Jesus making an audacious claim that he has the right to *interpret Israel's Old Testament Law*— to say what it means and why it's there in the first place! That's why Jesus says over and over again in that sermon, "You have

---

[11] Matt. 8:24–27; 9:6–7; 14:13–21; John 11:43

heard that it was said . . . but *I* say to you."[12] The emphasis is on
I. Jesus is making a radical claim that he is the nation of Israel's
rightful Legislator. What's more, look at *where* he's making
this claim: he's doing it very deliberately on top of a mountain,
and as every Israelite would have remembered, the great Law-
Giver (that's God) gave his people the Old Testament Law by
speaking to them *from the top of a mountain!*[13] You see? Jesus
was claiming for himself a breathtaking authority that no one
else would ever have dared to claim.

Then there was what he said at the tomb of a dead man to
Martha, the dead man's sister: "Your brother will rise again."
Martha apparently appreciated the reminder. "I know," she
answered. "He will rise again in the resurrection on the last
day." In other words, yes, yes, I know; thank you for your kind
sentiments; they're very comforting to me in this difficult sea-
son. But she didn't understand what Jesus meant. It would
have been astonishing enough if Jesus had said to her then,
"No, I mean he will rise again in a few minutes, when I tell
him to." But he said even more than that. He said, "I *am* the
resurrection. I *am* the life."[14] Don't walk by and miss that! It
wasn't just, I *can give* life. It was, I *am* life!

Really, what kind of man says things like that? What kind
of man hears his friend say to him in awe, "You are the Christ,
the Son of the Living God," and answers him with, essentially,
"Exactly. And it's God himself who told you that"? What kind
of man is asked by the rulers of his nation, "Are you the Christ,

---

[12] Matt. 5:21–44
[13] Ex. 19:16–20
[14] See John 11:23–25

the Son of the Blessed One?" and answers them back, "I am, and you will see the Son of Man seated at the right hand of Power, and coming with the clouds of heaven!"[15]

No ordinary man, that's for sure—no one who just wants to be recognized as a great teacher, or honored as a good person, or remembered as an influential philosopher. No, a person who talks about himself in those terms is claiming something far larger and more glorious and more world-shatteringly profound than any of that. And that's exactly what Jesus was doing, at least for those who were paying attention.

He was claiming to be Israel's—and humanity's—King.

---

[15] See Matt. 16:16–17; 26:63–64

3

King of Israel,
King of Kings

It was William Shakespeare, in 1597, who had Henry IV complaining about the duties of kingship. "How many thousands of my poorest subjects," the king lamented, "are at this hour asleep!"[1] He goes on to wonder why Sleep would rather live in the ramshackle hovels of the poor rather than in the palaces of a king, and how she can give her gift of rest to a soaked sailor boy being tossed around by the sea while denying it to a king in all his quiet comfort. "Uneasy lies the head that wears a crown!" Henry cries.[2]

That passage from Shakespeare is so arresting because it trades in a deep irony. Kings are supposed to have everything. They're rich and powerful; they have armies to protect them, fine palaces to shelter them, and servants to attend to their every whim. Who wouldn't want that? But if you know any history, then you know that Henry's right. Far from always affording an uninterrupted life of luxury and ease, kingship

---

[1] William Shakespeare, *The History of Henry IV*, Part 2, act 3, scene 1.
[2] Ibid.

often brings with it a good deal of unease and fear and even paranoia. Once you have the crown, the trick then is to keep it, and more than one monarch has realized too late just how difficult and dangerous that can be!

But for all that, I think you could say there's another kind of person whose head lies even more uneasily than a king's—and that's the man who *claims* to be a king when nobody else recognizes it. History has proven to be unkind to people who claim crowns they don't yet have. Yes, there's the slight chance of winning and winding up with the throne, but the downside is massive. If you're a failed would-be king, you don't get to just say "sorry" and go on about your life. More likely is that you wind up losing the head you intended to put the crown on in the first place!

One of the things that makes Jesus's life so captivating is the fact that he clashed—hard—with the ruling authorities of his day. He was a poor carpenter from a no-account, rural town in northern Israel who eventually found himself at odds not only with the rulers of his own people, but with the dominating Roman authorities in the region. If nothing else, that alone tells us that we're not dealing with a mere religious teacher, somebody who had a few nice proverbs about life and how to live it. We're also not dealing with merely a moral philosopher or ethical sage. No, as Jesus hung humiliated and dying on a Roman cross, the charge the Romans hung above his head read—in savage mockery of both him and the entire oppressed nation—"This Is Jesus, the King of the Jews."[3]

---

[3] Matt. 27:37

The story of Jesus is not the story of a good man. It is the story of a Claimant to the Throne.

The Throne of Israel, Empty No Longer

According to the Bible, Jesus began his public ministry on the day he was baptized in the Jordan River by a man known as John the Baptizer.

Now John had been preaching for months that people needed to repent of their sins (which simply means to turn away from them) because, he declared, the kingdom of God—that is, God's reign on the earth—was "at hand."[4] In other words, God's chosen King was about to be revealed, and the people desperately needed to prepare themselves for his coming. As a sign of their repentance, John asked the people to be dipped in the river's water, symbolizing their cleansing from sin and unrighteousness. The fact that Jesus was baptized in just that way is heavy with significance, and we'll think about that a little later. For now, though, it's enough to notice that when John the Baptizer saw Jesus walking toward him, he believed immediately that *this* was the one he'd been preaching about for so long. "Behold!" he said. "This is he of whom I said, 'After me comes a man who ranks before me, because he was before me.'"[5]

Here's the point: John knew the kingdom of God was about to be established on earth. That was his whole message. And now he was pointing to Jesus as the King of that

---

[4] Matt. 3:2
[5] John 1:29–30

kingdom. Even more significantly, this was far more than just a personal belief on John's part. According to Jesus himself, John was the last of the Old Testament prophets, the end of a centuries-long line of men whose greatest purpose had been to point the nation's eyes forward to the one true King whom God would eventually send to rescue them from their sin. Now John was declaring that the moment had come. The King was here.

You may have heard about what happened next. The Bible says that as Jesus came up out of the water following his baptism, "the Spirit of God [descended] like a dove and [came] to rest on him; and behold, a voice from heaven said, 'This is my beloved Son, with whom I am well pleased.'"[6] The significance of this is not *just* in the dove, or even in the voice that everyone understood rightly to be the voice of God. The significance is even more in what the voice said. As usual with the Bible, almost every word of it is packed with meaning, sometimes even multiple layers of meaning. But one detail in particular stands out. With the words "this is my beloved Son," God was investing Jesus with the ancient crown of the nation of Israel. Jesus was formally entering the office of King of the Jews.

How do we know that? Well, the phrase "Son of God" was a well-known title for Israel's King, and it had been so since the days of the Old Testament. The phrase had roots in Israel's exodus out of slavery in Egypt. When God heard the Israelites' prayers for rescue from the Egyptians, he confronted Egypt's Pharaoh with a threat. "Israel is my firstborn son," he said,

---

[6] Matt. 3:16–17

"and I say to you, 'Let my son go that he may serve me.'"[7] That was a declaration of fierce, discriminating love for the nation of Israel. It set them apart as *different* from all the other nations of the world. God was putting Pharaoh on notice that he would fight for Israel because he loved them, they were his son.

Years later, that designation, "God's son," was also given to Israel's king. God said about the great King David and his heirs, "I will be to him a father, and he shall be to me a son."[8] The symbolism is important: The King of Israel is called "God's son"—just like the nation—because he *represents* the whole nation in his very self. He stands as their representative, even their substitute before God, so that what happens to him as an individual can be said to happen to the nation as a whole. In that symbolic sense the king *is* Israel.

Once you understand that, you can see the awesome significance of what God said at Jesus's baptism. Yes, he was describing the Father-Son relationship that existed between him and Jesus (more on that later), but he was also declaring that Jesus was now formally entering into his work of representing Israel as their King. From that point on, he would stand before God as his people's Substitute, their Representative, even their Champion.

Jesus always knew the office of King was rightfully his. Yes, he often told people to keep that truth quiet, and once he even refused to let the people crown him as King. But that was not at all because he rejected the office; it was because he knew

---

[7] Ex. 4:22–23
[8] 2 Sam. 7:14

he was going to be a very different kind of King than what the people expected and wanted. He would take the crown on his own terms, not on the mistaken revolutionary terms of the people.

In fact, Jesus readily accepted royal acclamation *when people actually understood what they were acclaiming*. Matthew 16 tells of a night when Jesus, fresh out of another confrontation with Israel's rulers, asked his closest followers who the crowds thought he was. There were lots of answers. "Some say John the Baptist," his followers reported, "others say Elijah, and others Jeremiah or one of the prophets." Apparently Jesus was so astonishing that the people assumed he *had* to be someone returned from the grave! Whatever the people thought, though, Jesus was more interested in the thoughts of his own disciples. "But who do *you* say that I am?" he asked. The question put them on the spot, and it was a man named Simon who spoke first. "You are the Christ," he replied, "the Son of the Living God."

I think Simon actually meant even more than this, but at the very least he was acclaiming Jesus as Israel's King: You are the Anointed One (that's what *Christ* means in Greek), the Son of God, the King! And what was Jesus's response? He accepted the acclamation, and celebrated! "Blessed are you, Simon [son of] Jonah!" he said. "For flesh and blood has not revealed this to you, but my Father who is in heaven." Simon—whom Jesus immediately renamed Peter—had realized what Jesus already knew about himself. This was Israel's rightful King.[9]

---

[9] Matt. 16:13–20

In Luke 19, another story is told of when Jesus—just a week before he would be executed on the cross—made a dramatic and very public claim to kingship. Jesus and his disciples were making their way to Jerusalem for the annual Passover feast. It's likely that hundreds of thousands of people were pressing into the city that week, because it was the most important festival of the Jewish year. As they came closer to the city, Jesus sent some of his disciples ahead into a small village called Bethphage and told them to collect a donkey that would be waiting for them. The Bible says then that Jesus sat on the donkey and began the short journey from Bethphage to Jerusalem, with a large crowd following him. Here's what happened next:

> As he was drawing near—already on the way down the Mount of Olives—the whole multitude of his disciples began to rejoice and praise God with a loud voice for all the mighty works that they had seen, saying, "Blessed is the King who comes in the name of the Lord! Peace in heaven and glory in the highest!"[10]

> Most of the crowd spread their cloaks on the road, and others cut branches from the trees and spread them on the road. And the crowds that went before him and that followed him were shouting, "Hosanna to the Son of David! Blessed is he who comes in the name of the Lord! Hosanna in the highest!"[11]

---

[10] Luke 19:37–38
[11] Matt. 21:8–9

All of this was fraught with significance. Not only were the people waving branches and spreading their cloaks on the road in front of Jesus—a typical, symbolic response of submission to royalty—but they were also calling him King and declaring him to be the Heir of David! On top of that, they were quoting from an ancient song that the people used to greet their king as he approached the temple to offer sacrifices.[12]

The whole scene would have made quite a spectacle, and Jesus meant it to draw attention. Hearing the cries of the people and recognizing what they were saying, some of the Pharisees were scandalized and complained to Jesus. "Teacher," they said, "rebuke your disciples." Do you see what these temple authorities were doing? They wanted Jesus to agree with them that the people's cries of royal acclamation were inappropriate; they wanted him to deny kingship. But Jesus wouldn't do it. He answered, "I tell you, if these were silent, the very stones would cry out."[13] There would be no more delay. The time had come, and the King was arriving in his capital city.

The throne of Israel, unoccupied for some six hundred years, was empty no longer.

A Real King on a Real Throne with a Real History

It's hard for us today to grasp fully the significance of what was happening when Jesus rode into Jerusalem that day. I think we tend to assume that the people pressing around Jesus were simply playing out some sort of fevered religious drama, all to

---

[12] Ps. 118:26
[13] Luke 19:39–40

be forgotten when they finally came to their senses and went home. But those people weren't proclaiming a pretend religious king. They were proclaiming a *real* king who would sit on a *real* throne with a *real* history.

The nation of Israel had not always had a king. At the beginning of its history, when the nation was really not much more than an extended family, it was led first by a series of patriarchs and then by a long line of prophets and judges whom God raised up to rule and protect them. Eventually, though, the Israelites asked their prophet-leader Samuel to anoint a king for them. Samuel objected and warned them of the evils a king would bring, but the people insisted, and a king was crowned. The Israelite monarchy reached its height during the reign of King David, a shepherd boy from the village of Bethlehem who was (surprisingly) chosen by God to rule the nation. Blessed and guided by God himself, David enjoyed a meteoric rise in Israel until he finally took the throne in about 1000 BC. He united the twelve tribes of Israel under one crown, subjugated the nation's enemies, conquered Jerusalem, and made it the capital of the kingdom. Above all, God promised that he would establish David's dynasty forever.

David was remembered as the greatest of Israel's kings, so much so that the office itself came to be called "the Davidic kingship" and his seat "the Davidic throne." David himself was a celebrated warrior, a gifted musician, a sage, and even a poet. He wrote more than half the songs contained in Israel's book of Psalms, and he is still remembered as a model of faith and righteousness. It's not that David was perfect—far from it!—

but he had a deep love for God, a profound sense of his own guilt and neediness, and a strong faith that God would show him mercy and forgive him of his sins. The Bible even records that God declared David to be "a man after his own heart."[14]

When David died in about 970 BC, he was succeeded on Israel's throne by his son Solomon. Solomon's reign was in many ways even more glorious than his father's had been, at least at the beginning. Israel increased greatly in wealth and influence and seemed to be enjoying a golden age. Solomon died after a forty-year reign, though, and after that the Israelite monarchy descended into chaos. A civil war soon broke the nation into two different kingdoms—Israel in the north and Judah in the south—and the next few centuries saw a breathtaking descent of both nations' kings into idolatry and rank wickedness. One king of the south, Ahaz, is even recorded to have sacrificed his own son to a pagan god by burning him alive.

In the midst of all this, God sent prophets to warn both Israel and Judah to turn away from their sins and return to him. If they did so, God said, he would forgive them and restore them as a nation. If not, then judgment and death would follow. Neither nation repented. So in about 700 BC, the northern kingdom of Israel was invaded by the powerful Assyrian Empire, and its people were carried away into exile. The southern kingdom, Judah, survived for a little more than another century, until Nebuchadnezzar of Babylon invaded in 586 BC, destroyed Jerusalem and its temple, and deported its people to Babylon. As for the Davidic king, he was captured by the

---

[14] 1 Sam. 13:14

invading Babylonians and blinded. A hook was put through his nose, and he too was carted off to Babylon where, for the rest of his life, he was invited to take his meals at Nebuchadnezzar's table. Nice as that detail might sound, however, it was less an honor than it was a humiliation. The Davidic king of Israel was now nothing but a blind, wrecked dependent of the emperor of Babylon.

As the years passed, even after the Persian Empire defeated the Babylonians, and then the Greeks overthrew the Persians, and the Romans swallowed up the Greeks, Israel never managed to reestablish her independence or her throne. She remained an oppressed, dependent vassal of other nations. For six hundred years, the Davidic throne remained empty of a man to sit on it.

It did not, however, remain empty of hopes. That's because throughout the cataclysm of Israel's division, decline, and fall, the prophets continued foretelling a time when the Davidic dynasty would be restored. In fact, they told the Israelites that God would one day send a King who would rule from David's throne with perfect righteousness and justice. He would be anointed with the Spirit of God himself, he would turn the heart of the nation to worship God alone, and he would reign forever with wisdom, compassion, and love. Not only so, but God promised that the throne of David would not be a merely national throne. He would *universalize* its authority, and all the peoples of the earth would stream into Jerusalem to pay tribute to the King of Israel, the King of kings.[15]

---

[15] See, e.g., Isaiah 9; 11; Micah 5

All those prophecies must have seemed ridiculous as the Israelites watched their kings, one by one, fall into wickedness and under God's judgment. And they must have seemed like a cruel taunt as the last Davidic king begged for mercy just before the Babylonians put his eyes out. Yet, if the people had listened carefully to the prophecies, they would also have seen that this promised King the prophets spoke of didn't sound like just another man who would sit on the throne for a time and then die. He sounded like something much, much more. In fact, if they had listened, they would have heard their God promising not merely that he would *send* a king to Israel, but that he himself would *come* and *be* their King. Look at what the prophet Isaiah said about the birth of this great King:

> For to us a child is born,
>   to us a son is given,
> and the government shall be upon his shoulder.

Nothing too remarkable there, right? Sounds like any king. But read on:

> And his name shall be called
> Wonderful Counselor, Mighty God,
>   Everlasting Father, Prince of Peace.
> Of the increase of his government and of peace
>   there will be no end,
> [and he will sit] on the throne of David and over his
>   kingdom,
>   to establish it and to uphold it

with justice and with righteousness
>from this time forth and forevermore.[16]

Oh. Now that's no ordinary king. No ordinary king reigns "from this time forth *and forevermore*." No ordinary king has a government that increases *without end*. No ordinary king could be called, at least with a straight face, things like Wonderful Counselor, Everlasting Father, Prince of Peace. And above all, no one—king or not—can justifiably take to himself the name *Mighty God*. No one, that is, except . . . God.

Eyes Wide and Mind Filled with Awe

I always imagine Simon Peter saying those words—"You are the Christ, the Son of the Living God"—in a whisper, his eyes wide and his mind filled with awe. You see, I think it was all coming together for him. Yes, the kings of old had been styled "son of God," and everyone thought that was just a title. But it wasn't. It was God's way of pointing to the future, and to his own intention to sit *himself* on the throne of David. Just as the prophets had said, the great King would be "son of God" not just symbolically, not just in title, but in *reality*. God himself would be the King.

That's what Peter was realizing. This man sitting in front of him was the King, the Christ, the Anointed One of Israel, and therefore he was by title the "son of God." But he was also the *Son* of God. Not just the King of Israel, but the King of kings.

This man, Peter realized, was God.

---

[16] Isa. 9:6–7

4

The Great "I Am" . . .

The thought that Jesus was God did not occur to Peter out of the blue. Remember, he'd been with Jesus for months, watching as he performed miracles, healed people who couldn't otherwise be healed, and even raised people from the dead. Those events would have been enough to set anyone wondering.

But then there were other times that set the mind spinning—times when even the natural world itself seemed to bow down and defer to Jesus.

One such occasion was near the beginning of Jesus's public ministry. Word had gotten out about this man who could heal the sick and drive out demons, so massive crowds began to press around him. Jesus dealt with them patiently and kindly, spending hours casting out spirits and healing people of their diseases. But on this day, Jesus was tired. He had been healing and ministering for hours on the shore of the sea of Galilee, and seeing another enormous crowd pressing toward him, he and his disciples got into their boat and set sail for the other side.

The Sea of Galilee was very familiar to Jesus and his disciples. A good portion of Jesus's teaching and healing ministry took place in the ring of fishing villages that surrounded it, and some of his disciples—including Peter—had built careers fishing there before Jesus called them to follow him. The Sea of Galilee is actually not very big. In fact, it's not really a sea at all, but a freshwater lake. It's only about thirty-three miles all the way around, but one of its most notable characteristics is that it sits almost seven hundred feet below sea level and is surrounded by a series of deep ravines that channel wind into it at breakneck speeds. So besides being known for having a lot of fish, the Sea of Galilee was also famous for violent storms that would kick up regularly and without warning.

That's exactly what happened on this particular day, a few hours after Jesus and his followers set sail. As they made their way toward the middle of the lake, too far to turn back, one of those famous storms blew in. Apparently this wasn't just an average storm, though. Matthew, one of the disciples who was there and had seen these storms all his life, wrote that it was a "*great* storm," so unusually violent that he actually used the word *seismos* to describe it.[1] This wasn't just a storm, Matthew wants us to know; it was an earthquake on the water! So with the wind whipping down the ravines and into the lake, the disciples found themselves on a tiny boat being tossed around and swamped by massive waves in the middle of a violent sea.

The men, of course, were scared out of their wits. It was a natural response; the little boat could have been smashed and capsized easily, and no one would ever have heard from them again. So they were frightened. Jesus, on the other hand,

---

[1] Matt. 8:24

wasn't. He was asleep in the back of the boat. Not surprisingly, the disciples rushed to Jesus, woke him up, and said, "Save us, Lord; we are perishing." Well, those are the words Matthew recorded. Mark says it was, "Teacher, do you not care that we are perishing?" And Luke says it was, "Master, Master, we are perishing!"[2] The reality is that probably *lots* of things were being said at that moment, but one thing seems clear enough: the disciples knew they were in trouble. And they wanted Jesus to do something about it.

Now let's pause the story there for a moment, because it's interesting that they went to Jesus with this problem, isn't it? I mean, what exactly did these guys want Jesus to do? Somehow I doubt there was much of a real plan at all. The disciples were clearly impressed enough with Jesus that they assumed he could do *something*. But on the other hand, it's also clear that no one said, "You know what? We really should calm down. God's asleep in the back." So maybe they just expected him to protect them somehow while the storm raged, or to make the boat sail faster, or transport it in a moment to the other side. Who knows? But what's undeniably clear is that while they expected him to do something, they never for a moment expected him to do what he actually did.

Back to the story. The disciples in a panic rush to the back of the boat and shake Jesus awake, and he does something absolutely astonishing. He sits up, rubs his eyes maybe, and *talks to them*. "Why are you afraid, O you of little faith?"[3] I can only

---

[2] Matt. 8:25; Mark 4:38; Luke 8:24
[3] Matt. 8:26

wonder if one or two of the disciples—Peter especially—was tempted to say, "Why are we afraid? You have *got* to be kidding me!" But no one spoke, and the Bible says that Jesus, with amazing calm, stood up and "rebuked" the winds and the sea: "Peace!" he said. "Be still!"[4]

What a fascinating word! He "rebuked" them, like a father correcting a child. Have you ever tried to rebuke the wind or fuss at a storm? You might as well go out to the shore and try to reason with a hurricane for all the good it will do, and yet the Bible says that when Jesus told this storm to be still, it did. "The wind ceased," Mark writes, "and there was a great calm." All these disciples had seen storms come to an end before, even quickly. But it had never happened like this; even when the wind sometimes died suddenly, the water would remain choppy for quite some time before settling down. But this time the wind and waves just *stopped* and gave way to a preternatural calm. The disciples stood there marveling, dripping wet and looking with astonishment—from each other to Jesus and back to one another. The Bible doesn't say who finally asked the question, but I bet the others nodded, or at least shook their heads in silent, shared amazement: "Who then is this, that even the winds and the sea obey him?"[5]

Something Far beyond a Mere King

I wonder if Peter thought of that day when he answered Jesus's question by saying, "You are the Christ, the Son of the Living

---

[4] Mark 4:39
[5] Mark 4:41

God."[6] Some people think Peter wasn't saying anything more profound than that he recognized Jesus as the rightful King of Israel. It was a political statement, they say, and nothing more. I don't think that can possibly be right, though. Here's why: the last time the disciples had called Jesus "the Son of God," it was precisely because he had just done something *else* that catapulted him way beyond mere kingship. Not only so, but it was something that would have been especially memorable to Peter himself.

The circumstances were actually very similar to the time when Jesus calmed the storm. The disciples were in a boat on their way to the other side of the lake, and just like the last time, the winds began to blow and waves began to beat against the ship. The whole situation would have seemed completely familiar, except for one huge difference: this time, Jesus wasn't there.

On this particular day, Jesus had just fed over five thousand people from two fish and five loaves of bread, and afterward, he had sent his disciples ahead of him to the other side of the Sea of Galilee. Maybe they figured he would hire another boat or make his way around the lake on land, but either way, they set sail for the other side while Jesus himself stayed behind, finished ministering to the crowd, and then retired to the top of a nearby mountain to pray.

Meanwhile, out on the boat, the disciples were having a rough night. The boat was in trouble, the winds and waves were rising again, and they were afraid. The Bible says it was the fourth watch of the night—sometime between 3 a.m. and

---

[6] Matt. 16:16

6 a.m.—when they looked out and saw someone *walking toward them on the water*! Naturally their fear turned to terror, and they cried out, "It is a ghost!"

What happened next is one of the most famous events of Jesus's life—and perhaps also one of the heaviest with significance. Hearing the disciples' cries, Jesus called out to them, "Take heart; it is I. Do not be afraid!" Now stop and consider that sentence again, because in those few words, Peter apparently heard something that won his trust. Leaning forward, he called out, "Lord, if it is you, command me to come to you on the water." What an astonishing thing to say! You have to wonder if the other disciples looked at Peter as if he'd lost his mind! But he hadn't. There was something about what Jesus had just said that made it all click for Peter, and now he was about to put it to the test. Jesus must have known, too, what Peter was thinking, because he gave the invitation: "Come." And then, one foot at a time, Peter stepped out of the boat, stood on the water, and took a step. The Bible doesn't tell us how far he got, but before he made it to Jesus, Peter noticed the wind pressing against him and felt the water lapping at his legs. Taking his eyes off Jesus, he became frightened and began to sink. Then he cried out to Jesus to save him, and "immediately," the Bible says, Jesus reached out his hand, took hold of him, and brought him back to the boat. This time, Jesus didn't even have to give the command aloud— when he and Peter got back to the boat, the storm simply ceased.

That's when, Matthew tells us, "those in the boat worshiped him, saying, 'Truly you are the Son of God.'"[7]

---

[7] Matt. 14:26–33

Now what did they mean by that, calling him "the Son of God?" Did they mean that he was Israel's rightful king? Were they just bestowing a royal title on him that dozens of kings before him had used for themselves? No way! The disciples had just seen this man walk on water, call one of their own number to do the same, and calm a storm without a word. And think back, too, to what induced Peter to get out of the boat in the first place. What did he hear in Jesus's words, "Take heart; it is I," that led him not just to say, "Whew, OK, we can stop panicking now; it's Jesus," but actually to step onto the water? Why, all of a sudden, did he have such faith that Jesus was *entirely* in control of the whole situation?

The answer is that the sentence "It is I," though it may be good English grammar, does not convey . . . exactly . . . what Jesus said. What he said, literally, was "Take heart. *I am!*" That's what Peter heard that gave him such a deep confidence in Jesus. He heard his Lord saying not just, "Yoohoo! It's me, Jesus!" but rather taking for himself the ancient and famous name of Israel's Almighty God.

It all goes back, again, to the time of Israel's rescue from Egypt. One of the more amusing parts of that story is the argument Moses starts with God about why he is ill-equipped to do the job God was calling him to do. He tries several excuses— I'm not important enough, they won't believe me, I'm not a good enough public speaker—and each time God answers him and wipes the excuse away. One of the questions Moses asks, though, is what he should tell the people when they ask him what God's name is. God's answer was profoundly self-revealing: "God said to Moses, 'I AM WHO I AM.' And he said, 'Say this to the people of Israel, "I AM has sent me to you.""[8] Thus God revealed himself to be the transcendent, unbound God of the universe, the Source of all that is, the Author of being, the Creator and Ruler of the cosmos, the One who has always been, is now, and always shall be—the great "I AM."

That's what Peter heard that won his confidence. Jesus was taking the name of God for himself, and he was doing it *as he walked on the face of the sea*. The sea was the most powerful and fearsome force in creation, the ancient symbol of chaos and evil, the mythical home of rival gods. And here Jesus was subduing it, conquering it, ruling it, placing it literally under his feet. "Mightier than the thunders of many waters," the ancient song had said, "mightier than the waves of the sea, the LORD on high is mighty!"[9]

You see? When the disciples called Jesus "Son of God," they were proclaiming him to be something far beyond a mere king. They were saying he was God. He was the Creator. He was the great "I AM."

The Man Was Claiming to Be God

Sometimes people say the idea of Jesus being God was just a figment of the disciples' imagination, that Jesus never claimed that status for himself, and that after his death the disciples just made the story up—or, at best, misinterpreted their memories of all that had happened. But you don't even need to read the

---

[8] Ex. 3:14
[9] Ps. 93:4

Bible very carefully to see that Jesus did in fact claim that he was God, over and over again, and sometimes he didn't attempt to be subtle.

There was the time, for example, when he said, "I and the Father are one." There was also the time when Philip—getting a little impatient and missing the point entirely—said to him, "Lord, show us the Father," and Jesus replied, "Have I been with you so long, and you still do not know me, Philip? Whoever has seen me has seen the Father. How can you say, 'Show us the Father'?" There was also his response to the Jewish rulers at the end of his trial, when he told them, "From now on you will see the Son of Man seated at the right hand of Power and coming on the clouds of heaven." The high priest knew immediately what he was claiming; that's why he tore his robes and charged Jesus with nothing short of blasphemy. The man was claiming to be God.[10]

There was also the time when Jesus made a claim so over-the-top that the rulers actually picked up stones to kill him. The Bible says the situation was so dangerous that Jesus had to hide himself in order to get away. It all started when the Pharisees came up and started calling him names. "Are we not right in saying that you are a Samaritan and have a demon?" they said. It was a low insult, like accusing someone not only of having a demon but also of being from Washington, DC. (I kid! I kid!) Anyway, Jesus answered with, "I do not have a demon, but I honor my Father, and you dishonor me. . . . I say to you, if anyone keeps my word, he will never see death." The

---

[10] John 10:30; 14:8–9; Matt. 26:64

rulers, scandalized now, accused Jesus of massive arrogance: "Now we know that you have a demon! Abraham died, as did the prophets, yet you say, 'If anyone keeps my word, he will never taste death.' Are you greater than our father Abraham, who died? And the prophets died! Who do you make yourself out to be?"[11]

Jesus replied, "Your father Abraham rejoiced that he would see my day. He saw it and was glad." In other words, Abraham knew that God had promised to send a Savior, and he looked forward to it with joy. By this time the rulers were incensed, and confused. Jesus's claim that Abraham knew about him, and even that Jesus knew something of Abraham's emotional life, was just too much for them: "You are not yet fifty years old, and have you seen Abraham?"

Jesus's reply to that question rocked them. He said, "Truly, truly, I say to you, before Abraham was, I AM."[12]

There's that name again, and Jesus's use of it was deliberate and confrontational. How do we know that? Because otherwise what he said is simply bad grammar. Even if Jesus just wanted to say that he pre-existed Abraham somehow, he would have said, "Before Abraham was, *I was*." But by using the present tense—"I AM"—Jesus was clearly taking for himself, again, the unique and exclusive name of God. That's why they picked up stones in order to stone him. If he wasn't really God—and they didn't think he was—then he had committed the worst kind of blasphemy.

---

[11] John 8:48–53
[12] John 8:56–58

Face to Face with the Trinity

But of course it wasn't blasphemy. It was true, and Jesus had proved his claim to divinity over and over again. Once you understand that, you can start to see new layers of significance in Jesus's insistence that he was the Son of God. It wasn't just a royal title; it was also a claim that Jesus was equal to God in status and character and honor. John explains: "This was why the Jews were seeking all the more to kill him, because . . . he was even calling God his own Father, making himself equal with God."[13]

But there's even more to the phrase than that, because with it Jesus was not just taking a royal title, and not even just saying he was equal to God, but also describing a unique and exclusive *relationship* between himself and God the Father. "No one knows the Son except the Father," he once said, "and no one knows the Father except the Son and anyone to whom the Son chooses to reveal him."[14] Another time he explained,

> Whatever the Father does, that the Son does likewise. For the Father loves the Son and shows him all that he himself is doing. . . . For as the Father raises the dead and gives them life, so also the Son gives life to whom he will. The Father judges no one, but has given all judgment to the Son, that all may honor the Son, just as they honor the Father. Whoever does not honor the Son does not honor the Father who sent him.[15]

---

[13] John 5:18
[14] Matt. 11:27
[15] John 5:19–23

Do you see? Jesus the Son of God was claiming to be God himself, and yet also to be in a unique, exclusive, and entirely harmonious relationship with God the Father.

Now how can that be?

How can Jesus *be* God and yet be *in relationship with* God the Father at the same time? Here we come face to face with the Christian doctrine of the Trinity—which is just a linguistic smashing together of the word *Tri-Unity*. Maybe you've heard the word *Trinity*. Maybe you've even heard Christians talk about how God the Father, God the Son, and God the Holy Spirit are all distinct from each other—three different persons—and yet they are all one God. Not three gods! No, the Bible is clear from page one that there is only one God, and yet that one God exists in three distinct persons.

What I hope you can see here is that Christians didn't just make up the idea of the Trinity out of whole cloth. They defined it, described it, taught it, and defended it *because they saw it in the Bible*. They heard it in the way Jesus talked about himself, about his relationship with the Father, and about the Holy Spirit. Here, very briefly, is a summary of what they heard as they listened to Jesus:

1. They heard Jesus affirm that there is only *one* God.[16]
2. They heard Jesus say that he himself is God, that his Father is God, and (later) that the Holy Spirit is God.[17]
3. Finally, they heard Jesus make clear that he, his Father, and the Spirit are *not* the same person, but rather distinct

---

[16] E.g., Mark 12:29
[17] E.g., John 5:18; 8:58; Luke 12:10

from one another and in unique, exclusive relationship with each other.[18]

Now you may look at those three statements and say, "I don't understand how all three of those can be true all at the same time and in the same way." Well, to be perfectly honest, I don't either! And neither does any other Christian. But my understanding or lack of it is not the point. As a Christian, I believe Jesus, and Jesus taught those three things, and so I believe them—all of them, at the same time, even if they don't finally and fully reconcile in my mind.

The bottom line is that there's no logical contradiction in those three statements, and besides, I am well aware that my mind is not infinite. There are lots of things about this world that I don't fully understand, so it's not hard for me to imagine that there are going to be an infinite number of things that can fit into God's infinite mind that just don't fit into mine. What I know for sure is that Jesus taught that there's one God, that he and his Father and the Holy Spirit are all God, and that he and his Father and the Spirit are not the same person but are all in relationship with each other. And I, along with Christians throughout the centuries, call that whole complex reality Tri-Unity, or *Trinity*.

The Only Way

Here's the point: Once you begin to understand that Jesus is in fact God, and that he is in a unique and exclusive relationship

---

[18] Note the relationship, for example, in John 14:16–17.

with God the Father, you also begin to understand that if you want to know the God who created you, then you need to know Jesus. There's just no other way.

This is why it's such good news that Jesus is not only the great "I AM." He is also fully and forever *one of us*.

5

. . . Is One of Us

Early in Christian history, a certain group of people denied that Jesus was really human. The evidence for Jesus's divinity was so strong, they said, that he couldn't possibly also be human. Perhaps he was just God with skin, perhaps something in between God and human, but there was no way that he could really be *one of us*. The people who denied Jesus's humanity eventually became known as *Docetists*. The name comes from the Greek word *doke*, which means "seems," and it was a fitting word for their position: Jesus wasn't really human, they said; he only *seemed* to be.

Other Christians quickly declared that Docetism was wrong. They read the Bible, and they understood that Jesus didn't just *seem* human, as if he were an illusion or a ghost, or as if God had just taken on the *look* of humanity but not its reality. No, if the Bible could be believed, then Jesus *was* human—in every way. These Christians in no way denied his divinity. They were convinced that Jesus was the Son of God, the Creator of the world, the great "I AM." But they were just as convinced that the great "I AM" had, incredibly, become one of us.

Not Just a Visitor

The stories of Jesus's life are chock full of evidence that Jesus was human, just like us. The Bible tells us that he got hungry, he got thirsty, he got tired, and he even got sleepy (remember the nap in the boat?). He wasn't what the Greeks and Romans thought of as "a god," some Olympian figure who would sometimes take on human form but never really had to *be* human, with all the challenges and even weaknesses that come with it. No, Jesus was really human, and he had to live with all those things just like you and I do.

That means that when he didn't eat enough, he became hungry. When he didn't sleep enough, he got tired. When the soldiers pushed the thorns into the skin of his scalp and drove the nails into his wrists, it hurt. When his friend died, he mourned and wept—even when he intended just a few minutes later to bring his friend back to life! He even became weak. The Bible tells us that after the Romans beat Jesus with whips, they had to conscript a man who was watching to carry Jesus's cross to the place of execution. And then there's the most profound evidence of all: Jesus died. He didn't just *seem* to die, or die halfway, or *kind of* die, or even die *in a sense*. True, the story doesn't end with Jesus's death, but there's no getting around it: he died.[1]

It's crucial that we understand that Jesus really was human, because it means that he was not just a visitor to our world. That would be a neat thing, in its own way, wouldn't it—for the great Other to come for a visit? But that's not what hap-

---

[1] Matt. 4:2; 8:24; 27:50; John 19:2; 11:35; 19:33

pened. What really happened is magnitudes of awesomeness beyond that. God the Creator, the great Other, the great "I AM," became human.

Christians call that reality the *incarnation*, which is a Latin term that means "enfleshment," the idea being that, in Jesus, God took on human flesh. We have to be careful, though, because that word could be a little misleading. Understood wrongly, it could give you the idea that Jesus's humanity was just a matter of skin—that God put on a human hide like you or I might put on a coat, and that was the extent of Jesus's humanity. But that would take us too close to Docetism, the idea that Jesus only *seemed* human. Whatever else you think, surely we can agree that the essence of humanity is not skin; it's deeper than that, and the Bible says that Jesus was human all the way to the core, in every way. That's why Christians through the centuries settled on describing Jesus as being "fully God and fully human." He isn't part God and part human, or a mixture of God and human, or even something halfway between God and human.

He is God.

And he is human.

And here's the thing: that's not just a temporary reality. Jesus is human now, and he will never be anything *other than* human—forever. A few years ago, I was having breakfast with a friend, and that truth came crashing into my consciousness during a spirited conversation about (hang with me here) alien life-forms. My friend and I had been arguing for a while about whether other intelligent life could exist in the universe, whether the Bible had anything to say about it, what it would mean if they did, etc., etc., when this question came up: if aliens exist, and if they are sinners like we are, could God save them and how would he do it?

My immediate answer was, "Of course he could! Jesus would just incarnate as a Martian, die for their sins, too, and that would be that! Then he could make a decision about the Klingons." The answer made sense at the time, but do you see why it was wrong? My friend shook his head and said, "No, Greg. Jesus is human. Always and forever. He'll never be anything else but human." I had never thought about it like that.

In a Word, He Loved

That was an off-the-wall conversation, to be sure, but the realization that resulted from it was amazing to me: Jesus is human, *and he always will be*. Right now, sitting on the throne of the universe, is a human being. When he judges the entire world, he will be human. For all eternity, age after age, God is human and always will be. He didn't just put on human skin, like a coat, only to take it off again when he got home to heaven. He became a man—heart, soul, mind, and strength— a man!

Just imagine for a minute how much the Son of God must have loved human beings to decide that, yes, he would become a human forever. He had existed for all eternity, the second person of the Trinity, in perfect and harmonious and beautiful relationship with God the Father and God the Holy Spirit, and yet he decided to become human, and he knew when he did it that he would never be not-human again. There's only one thing that would lead the Son of God to do that: he deeply loves us, and you can see that fact in every detail of his life.

Over and over again, the biblical writers tell us that Jesus was moved by compassion for those around him. The reason he stayed so long healing people, Matthew tells us, is because he had compassion on them. The reason he taught the people, Mark says, is because he had compassion on them. When he looked out over a crowd of four thousand people who hadn't eaten a good meal in days, he told his disciples, "I have compassion on the crowd because they have been with me now three days and have nothing to eat. And I am unwilling to send them away hungry, lest they faint on the way." When he came ashore and was greeted by a throng of people eager to be taught by him, "he had compassion on them, because they were like sheep without a shepherd. And he began to teach them many things."[2]

He once came upon the funeral of a young man who had just died—the only son of a widow who now had no means to support herself. Here's what happened: "When the Lord saw her, he had compassion on her and said to her, 'Do not weep.' Then he came up and touched the bier, and the bearers stood still. And he said, 'Young man, I say to you, arise.' And the dead man sat up and began to speak, and Jesus gave him to his mother."[3]

When he arrived at the house of his friend Lazarus and saw the dead man's sister weeping, "he was deeply moved in

---

[2] Matt. 15:32; Mark 6:34; see Matt. 6:34; 14:1
[3] Luke 7:13–15

his spirit and greatly troubled." "Where have you laid him?" Jesus asked, and they took him to the tomb. The Bible says that there, in front of the grave of his friend, "Jesus wept." No one was under any illusion that this expression of emotion was anything other than the result of grief and love. The Jews who were there shook their heads and said, "See how he loved him!"[4]

Do you see the kind of person Jesus was? He wasn't the kind of hard, calculating man that often makes claims of kingship and godhood for himself. No, Jesus was a man whose heart beat with deep love for those around him. He enjoyed spending time with the outcasts of society, eating with them and even attending their parties, because, he said, "Those who are well have no need of a physician, but those who are sick. I have not come to call the righteous but sinners to repentance."[5] He took little children in his arms, hugged them and blessed them, and even rebuked his disciples when they tried to keep them away because he was too busy. He embraced his disciples, told jokes, spoke people's names tenderly, encouraged and forgave and strengthened and reassured and restored. In a word, he *loved*.

You see? Even when he did extraordinary things—things that only God himself could do—he did them with a deeply human tenderness and compassion and love. He not only *was* human; he showed us what God intended humanity to be, all along.

---

[4] John 11:33–36
[5] Luke 5:31–32

Why Did God the Son Become a Man?
Because We Needed Him To

For all that, however, it's important to realize that Jesus didn't come *only* to show us authentic, God-intended humanness. No, Jesus became human because we *needed* him to do so. We needed someone to represent us before God and be our substitute. That's ultimately why Jesus came—to be a loving Warrior King who would save his beloved people.

Part of what Jesus was doing when he became human, therefore, was *identifying* with us, becoming one with us so that he could represent us. That's why Jesus insisted on the first day of his public ministry that John the Baptizer baptize him. At first, John objected, because he knew that his baptism was for repentance—meaning that it was for those who knew they were sinners and were making a choice to turn away from their sins—and he knew that Jesus, as the sinless Son of God, had no need for that. Jesus didn't rebuke John for his resistance; he knew just as well as John did that he didn't need to repent of anything. But that's not why he wanted to be baptized, so he said to John, "Let it be so now, for thus it is fitting for us to fulfill all righteousness."[6] In other words, Jesus was saying, "You're absolutely right, John. I don't need a baptism of repentance, but I have another, different, purpose in mind for this, and right now it is good and right for us to do this." You see, Jesus was being baptized not because he needed to repent of any sin but in order to make it clear that he was fully and completely identifying with sinful human beings. He was

---

[6] Matt. 3:15

meeting us where we are, planting himself firmly in our shoes, taking his place among us, and locking arms—for better or worse—with a sinful, broken humanity.

And you remember from earlier what came next, right? It was the voice from heaven, identifying Jesus as the *eternal* Son of God, and also installing him as the *royal* son of God, the King of Israel. Oh, there's still more to see in those words that came from heaven, but for now it's enough to see that *this* is why it was right for Jesus to be baptized with a bunch of sinners: he was taking on the office of being their Substitute, their King, even their Champion.

The Battle Begins

Mark writes that "the Spirit immediately drove him out into the wilderness. And he was in the wilderness forty days, being tempted by Satan."[7] This was a fitting next step. Having taken up the kingship, having identified himself irrevocably with sinners, King Jesus rises to take up their ancient fight for them, to adopt their lost cause and win it for them. So he goes out into the wilderness to confront his people's mortal enemy, and the battle that will rage for the rest of history—between Satan the great Accuser and Jesus the great King—begins.

Even the seemingly insignificant details of the story point us to the realization that King Jesus was fighting again the same battle that his people, the nation of Israel, had already lost. Think about the fact that the temptation took place in the wilderness; the wilderness is where Israel wandered for a

---

[7] Mark 1:12–13

generation, and failed so disastrously. And the forty days of fasting? It was forty years that Israel wandered in the desert, so Jesus symbolically endures the same—one day for every year. What's happening here is unmistakable. Having taken the crown, Jesus was now taking up the fight on his people's behalf.

Matthew tells us more than anyone else about Satan's tempting of Jesus. It was one of the most dramatic moments of Jesus's life. As Satan presents Jesus with three temptations, the intensity of the situation spirals into the stratosphere. Even the geography of the temptations speaks to this: The first one takes place on the ground of the desert, the second at the pinnacle of the temple, and the last one at the top of a very high mountain. It's as if the very altitude of the clash increases right along with its intensity.

Satan's first temptation doesn't seem like much of a test at all. "If you are the Son of God," Satan said, "command these stones to become loaves of bread." Now keep in mind that Jesus had been fasting for over a month—probably taking only enough nourishment to survive—so he would have been very hungry. Moreover, Jesus would soon do miracles that were far and away more incredible than turning some stones into bread, so the act would have been easy for him. If that's true, then why would it have been wrong for him to do it? The answer comes in how he replied to Satan: "It is written, 'Man shall not live by bread alone, but by every word that comes from the mouth of God.'" The point was not whether Jesus would just *do something, anything* that Satan suggested. It was whether Jesus would—like Israel before him—demand his own comfort and relief *right now*, or whether he would submit to the path of humility and suffering that God his Father had placed before him. Where humans had sinned over and over by demanding instant gratification, King Jesus trusted God to sustain and care for him.

After Jesus had defeated his first temptation, Satan then took him to Jerusalem and set him at the very highest point of the temple. The height would have been dizzying. "If you are the Son of God," he said, "throw yourself down, for it is written, 'He will command his angels concerning you,' and 'On their hands they will bear you up, lest you strike your foot against a stone.'" Again, what Satan said made so much sense, and now he was even quoting Scripture to Jesus! But just as before, the temptation here was for Jesus to demand his own way instead of God's—to demand, like Israel had done so often, that God *prove* his care in a particular way. Do you see? Satan was tempting Jesus to exalt himself above his Father by trying to force his Father's hand instead of taking his Father at his word. Jesus refused to do that, and answered Satan, "Again it is written, 'You shall not put the Lord your God to the test.'" In other words, you shall not doubt him by demanding proof of his care. Trust him, take him at his word, and he will care for you in his own way and in his own time.

The third temptation was also the most brazen. Taking Jesus to the top of a very high mountain, Satan showed him all the kingdoms of the world and their glory. And then he made this offer: "All these I will give you," he said, "if you will fall down and worship me!" What an audacious and insidious offer! The creature was asking his Creator to bow down and worship him, and in return offering him everything his Father had already promised him—but *apart* from the path of suffering on which Jesus's Father had set him. Israel had faced this test over and over again—the temptation to create alliances with powerful neighbors, to scheme and disobey, all to gain safety and even glory for themselves from someone else's hand, rather than from God's. Time and again, Israel failed that temptation; King Jesus did not. He ended the fight, telling the Tempter, "Be gone, Satan! For it is written, 'You shall worship the Lord your God and him only shall you serve.'"[8]

Can you see what Jesus was doing here as he confronted Satan in the wilderness? He was picking up a fight for righteousness and obedience that his people Israel had long ago lost completely. The three temptations that Satan throws at him—distrust God, force God's hand, fail to worship God—were the famous failings of the nation of Israel. They were winners for Satan, and so he threw them now at Israel's King. But this time, Satan fails. King Jesus matches him step for step. Israel's Champion refights the battle for his people, and he wins!

Luke records that "when the devil had ended every temptation, he departed from him until an opportune time."[9] It was not yet over, but the battle for humanity's soul—ages and ages in the making—was now well and truly joined.

---

[8] Matt. 4:3–10
[9] Luke 4:13

6

The Triumph of the Last Adam

Conflicts often have roots that go deep into history. If you read the headlines about wars, battles, and conflicts taking place on any given day, you'll find that those events rarely materialize out of nothing. Sometimes the origins of conflicts go back centuries or even longer.

So it was with Jesus and Satan. When Jesus met and defeated the great Accuser in the wilderness, it was a culminating moment in a millennia-long conflict, one involving all of humanity. Actually, it was the beginning of the end of that conflict. For centuries Satan had been opposing God and his plans in the world, but now he came face to face with the One who would defeat him—and decisively. It's not that Satan was unaware of who Jesus was; two of the temptations specifically pressed on his identity as the Son of God. Yet even knowing that, Satan still somehow believed he could get Jesus to sin. And why not? Every other human being in history had fallen to his temptations. Why not this one, too? Perhaps God had made a mistake by becoming human like this, by taking human flesh, human weakness, human limitations. Maybe God had finally become . . . breakable.

By the end of that first encounter with Jesus, though, Satan must have realized that was an empty hope. In fact, seeing that his best tactics had failed him, you have to wonder if he went away knowing the end was coming soon. You have to wonder if he remembered the voice of God promising him, so many millennia ago, "When the King comes, yes, you will bruise his heel, but he will crush your head."[1]

It must have made him long for the days when the war against God seemed to be going better.

He Wanted to Dethrone God

The Bible doesn't spend much time talking about Satan. Its focus is on God, his relationship with human beings, their rebellion and sin against him, and his plan to rescue and forgive them. But Satan is there all the same, the Tempter and Accuser of humanity, the greatest Enemy of God and his plans. We aren't told much about his origins, but the Bible contains hints here and there of where he came from. Above all, it's clear that Satan is in no way a sort of *anti-God,* equal in power but just opposite in character from God himself. In other words, he's never presented as the yang to God's yin.

Actually the prophets of the Old Testament indicate that originally Satan was an angel created by God to serve him just like all other angels. Here's how Ezekiel describes him:

---

[1] See Gen. 3:15

You were the signet of perfection,

> full of wisdom and perfect in beauty.

You were in Eden, the garden of God;

> every precious stone was your covering,

sardius, topaz, and diamond,

> beryl, onyx, and jasper,

sapphire, emerald, and carbuncle;

> and crafted in gold were your settings
>
> and your engravings.

On the day that you were created

> they were prepared.

You were an anointed guardian cherub.

> I placed you; you were on the holy mountain of God;
>
> in the midst of the stones of fire you walked.

You were blameless in your ways

> from the day you were created,
>
> till unrighteousness was found in you.[2]

When you read the book of Ezekiel, it's obvious that this statement is talking most directly about the king of a city called Tyre. The whole thing is prefaced by God telling Ezekiel, "Raise a lamentation over the king of Tyre."[3] But then again, the Old Testament prophecies are wonderfully mysterious messages, and sometimes there's more going on than what appears right on the surface. That's the case here. From the very first words of this message, it's clear that Ezekiel's not talking about *just* the king of Tyre. After all, what would it

---

[2] Ezek. 28:12–15
[3] Ezek. 28:12

even mean to say that this guy—the ruler of a rich but still relatively obscure coastal city in the ancient Near East—was *in Eden*, that he was *an anointed guardian cherub*, and that he was *on the holy mountain of God*? It wouldn't make sense at all; even as poetry, it would be overkill to the point of absurdity and poetic failure.

Clearly something else is happening here, and the effect is almost cinematic. It's as if the face of the evil king of Tyre is flickering in and out with another face—the face of one who stands behind Tyre's evil, who drives it and encourages it and whose character it reflects. Do you see what Ezekiel is doing there? As a way of heightening the power of his prophecy against the king of Tyre, he's giving us a glimpse of the one who, above all, embodies rebellion against God—Satan. So Ezekiel goes on to describe Satan's fall from his high position: "Your heart was proud because of your beauty; you corrupted your wisdom for the sake of your splendor. I cast you to the ground; I exposed you before kings, to feast their eyes on you."[4] Another prophet, Isaiah, describes Satan's sin like this: "How you are fallen from heaven, O Day Star, son of Dawn! How you are cut down to the ground, you who laid the nations low! You said in your heart, 'I will ascend to heaven; above the stars of God I will set my throne on high; . . . I will ascend above the heights of the clouds; I will make myself like the Most High.'"[5]

More than anything else, Satan's sin was pride. For all his otherworldly splendor and beauty, he wasn't content to be

---

[4] Ezek. 28:17
[5] Isa. 14:12–14

what God had created him to be. He wanted more. He wanted to be, as Isaiah said, "like the Most High." He wanted to dethrone God.

Is it any wonder, then, that when Satan decided to attack human beings, to tempt them to rebel against God and make their own way, he did it by promising them that if they would just throw off his authority, they too could *be like God*?

A Living Reminder That God Is King

The story picks up at the very beginning of the Bible, in the book of Genesis, and it quickly becomes clear why humanity needs Jesus. By successfully tempting the first humans to sin, Satan strikes a blow that he thinks will ruin humanity beyond repair, and at the same time will strike not only at God's heart, but also at the very foundation of his throne.

The word *genesis* means "beginning," and that's exactly what the book describes. In its first chapters it tells of how God created the entire world—the land, the sea, the birds and animals and fish—simply by speaking them into existence, and it makes clear that when he had finished, his creation was good. It also tells of how God capped his creative work by making human beings. The first man was not just another animal. He was special, created by God "in his image," the Bible says, and clearly set above the rest of creation. Humanity had a special place in God's heart, and in his plan. Here's how Genesis describes God's creation of the first man: "Then the Lord God formed the man of dust from the ground and breathed into his nostrils the breath of life, and the man became a living creature."[6] The Hebrew word that stands behind the phrase "the man" is actually *adam*, which naturally becomes the man's name—Adam.

God was kind to Adam right from the beginning. He placed him in a special area of the earth called Eden, in which God had planted a garden. It was a beautiful place through which a river flowed and in which grew "every tree that is pleasant to the sight and good for food." Even more, in the center of the garden stood two special trees, the Tree of Life and the Tree of the Knowledge of Good and Evil. Adam's life in the garden was good, but so far it was incomplete. Adam needed a companion, and God knew it: "Then the LORD God said, 'It is not good that the man should be alone; I will make him a helper fit for him.'" So, God did what any of us would quite naturally do at this point: he made Adam name all the animals![7]

Now if you're wondering what on earth is going on here, you're not alone! That plot twist in the story has left more than a few people scratching their heads. Most people, even long-time Christians, just chalk it up to a nice, cute children's story thrown in, a kind of commercial break before the story picks up again with the creation of Eve. But if you want to understand the Bible, one important principle to remember is that it is never random. The story of Adam naming the animals does a couple of important things. For one, God is giving Adam an important object lesson. As all of the animals and birds and fish and insects parade by him, and Adam calls out words

---

[6] Gen. 1:27; 2:7
[7] Gen. 2:8–10, 18

like "Tiger!" "Rhinoceros!" and "Mosquito!" he comes to the realization that none of those creatures is going to work as a companion to him. None of them are like him.

Once the point is made, God puts Adam in a deep sleep and, taking one of his ribs from his side, God creates the first woman, to be Adam's companion. Imagine Adam's excitement when he woke up and saw her standing there! She was perfect! Especially after seeing how badly the blue whale, the giraffe, and the beetle would have failed as companions, Adam exclaimed, "This *at last* is bone of my bones and flesh of my flesh; she shall be called Woman, because she was taken out of Man."[8] That's part of why God had Adam name all those animals. He wanted him to know, without any second-guessing, that the woman standing before him was created specifically for him, even in the most intimate way *from him*.

There was something else happening with the naming of the animals, too. God must have delighted to watch Adam doing his work, but it wasn't all fun and games. It was also God's way of communicating to Adam that he had a job to do in the world. As the capstone of creation—the only creature made in God's image—Adam was to be the ruler of God's world. To name something is a way to exert authority over it, much as a mother and father have the privilege of naming their child. So in giving names to the animals, Adam was actually exerting authority over them. He was carrying out his job as the vice-regent of God's creation, under God himself.

That fact is significant, too, when we realize that as soon

---

[8] Gen. 2:23

as Adam sees the woman, he names her—"she shall be called Woman"—and later the Bible says that he named her again—"The man called his wife's name Eve." You can see what God is doing here. He's instituting a whole system of authority in which Adam is given authority over Eve, and the two of them together as husband and wife are given authority over creation, and all of it is meant to reflect the reality that God sits enthroned above it all. That's at least part of what God meant when he said he would create the man and the woman "in his image." An image or statue was often used by conquering kings to remind those who had been conquered of who ruled them now. Placed on a high point so it would be visible from almost anywhere in the region, it communicated to the people, "This is your king." So it was with Adam and Eve in God's creation. Whatever else the idea of being created in God's image included, it meant that the humans were to stand in the world as a reminder to all the universe that God is King. Even as they were to have authority over creation, they were to do so as the representatives of the great King, God himself.

All of which must have galled Satan to no end.

The Devastation Was Near Total

Satan's attack on the humans was exquisitely calculated to overthrow everything God had done in the garden. You see, he wasn't just interested in getting one little human to commit one little sin against God. He wanted to upend every structure of authority, every symbol of kingship and rule that God had instituted. He wanted the whole structure of creation—from bottom to top—overturned, and he wanted God humiliated.

The Bible says that God had told Adam and Eve that they were free to eat from any tree in the garden of Eden except one—the Tree of the Knowledge of Good and Evil. That tree is significant for a few reasons. For one thing, it was a reminder to the humans that their authority over creation was derived and limited; it was not sovereign. When God told them not to eat its fruit, he wasn't being capricious. He was rightly reminding Adam and Eve that he was their King, that though they had been honored as the vice-regents of creation, he was Creator and Lord. That's why the punishment God promised for disobedience was so severe: "In the day that you eat of it you shall surely die."[9] For Adam and Eve to disobey that command would have been an attempt to throw off God's authority—in essence, a declaration of war against their King.

The tree was significant for another reason, too. The first readers of Genesis would have realized immediately that "to know good and evil" was the typical job of a judge in Israel. It meant that the judge would discern good from evil and then hand down decisions that reflected those realities. The Tree of the Knowledge of Good and Evil, therefore, was a place of judgment. It was where Adam should have exercised his authority as the protector of God's garden, making sure that nothing evil ever entered it, and if it did, making sure that evil thing was judged and cast out.

It was right here—at the Tree of Judgment, the reminder

---

[9] Gen. 2:17

to Adam of God's ultimate rule—that Satan made his attack. Taking the form of a snake, he confronted Eve with the suggestion that she break God's command and eat the fruit. Here's how Genesis describes the encounter:

> Now the serpent was more crafty than any other beast of the field that the LORD God had made.
>
> He said to the woman, "Did God actually say, 'You shall not eat of any tree in the garden'?" And the woman said to the serpent, "We may eat of the fruit of the trees in the garden, but God said, 'You shall not eat of the fruit of the tree that is in the midst of the garden, neither shall you touch it, lest you die.'" But the serpent said to the woman, "You will not surely die. For God knows that when you eat of it your eyes will be opened, and you will be like God, knowing good and evil." So when the woman saw that the tree was good for food, and that it was a delight to the eyes, and that the tree was to be desired to make one wise, she took of its fruit and ate, and she also gave some to her husband who was with her, and he ate.[10]

It was a tragic outcome and, at least at that moment, an almost total victory for Satan. Not only did he convince God's beloved humans to disobey him—by promising them what he himself wanted all along, "to be like God!"—but he did what he had set out to do from the very beginning: he upended the entire authority structure of creation.

Here's how: have you ever wondered why Satan came to

---

[10] Gen. 3:1–6

Eve with his temptation instead of to Adam? Even though Adam was the one given authority, and even though the rest of the Bible consistently blames Adam for the sin, Satan actually came to Eve first. Why? It wasn't because Satan somehow thought Eve would be an easier target. No, it was because his whole aim was to humiliate God and to overthrow his authority. And he wanted to do it as convincingly and as profoundly as possible. Therefore he didn't just want Adam to sin against God; he wanted Eve to subvert Adam into rebelling against God. But then there's even more: did you ever wonder why Satan came to the humans in the form of a snake? Why not come as another human, or if it had to be an animal, a giraffe or a prairie dog? Same reason: it's because Satan wanted the overthrow of God's authority to be total and complete. So he came as an animal *over whom Adam and Eve had authority*, and also as (symbolically speaking) *the lowest of the animals*, the snake. You see? The structures of authority fell like dominoes. A lowly animal tempted the woman, who subverted the man, who declared war against God.

The devastation was near total. Adam had failed in his tasks in every imaginable way. Instead of judging the Serpent for his evil at the Tree of the Knowledge of Good and Evil, he joined Satan's rebellion against God. Instead of protecting the garden and casting the Serpent out of it, he surrendered the garden to him. Instead of believing God's word and acting on that belief, he doubted God's word and gave his trust to Satan instead. Instead of submitting to God and faithfully executing his role as vice-regent, he decided he wanted to take the high crown for himself. Just like Satan before him, he decided he wanted to be "like God."

A Nightmare of a World

The results of Adam's sin were cataclysmic. With the world now in rebellion against the Creator, God executed justice and cursed the man and his wife, as well as the one who had tempted them. For the man and woman, he decreed that life would no longer be a paradise for them. It would be hard, and grueling, and painful. Childbirth would be painful, work would be toilsome, and the earth would be stingy with its goods and fruits. Worst of all, the intimate relationship Adam and Eve had enjoyed with God was now severed; they were cast out of the garden of Eden forever, and the way back was closed and guarded by an angel with a burning sword. That was the deepest meaning of God's promise of death for disobedience. Yes, Adam and Eve would die physically in time, but the more important death they suffered was *spiritual* death. They were cut off from God, the Author of life, and their souls died under the weight of their disobedience.

It's important to understand that Adam and Eve's sin did not affect *only* them. It also affected all their descendants. Thus the next few chapters of the Bible show how sin progressed among human beings as the generations passed. Adam and Eve's son Cain murders his brother Abel out of pride and jealousy, and from there sin begins to take a stronger and stronger hold on the hearts of humanity. Cain's descendants do make some progress culturally—they build a city and manage to advance technologically and artistically—but the Bible's story is clear that human beings are becoming more and more hardened in their sin, more and more committed to rebellion against God, immorality, and violence. One of Cain's descendants even boasts that he has killed a man for simply wounding him, and brags that he will avenge himself seventy-seven-fold against anyone who dares harm him. Sin had created a nightmare of a world.[11]

At the same time, the physical effects of God's death sentence against Adam and Eve—that their bodies would return to the earth as dust—were being executed not just against them, but . . . *against all humanity*. There's an amazing chapter in Genesis which gives a list of Adam's descendants and how long each of them lived. What's extraordinary about it—other than how long people lived then—is how each entry ends. Time and time again, the records of the people's lives end with the phrase, "and he died." Adam lived 930 years, and he died. Seth lived 912 years, and he died. Enosh . . . died. Kenan . . . died. Mahalalel and Jared and Methuselah . . . all died. Just as God had said, death was reigning among humans.[12]

Do you see the significance of that? When Adam sinned, he did not do so merely as an individual—nor did he suffer the consequences of his sin merely as an individual. When he sinned, he did so as the representative of all who would come after him. That's why Paul could say in the New Testament that "one trespass led to condemnation for all men" and "by the

---

[11] Gen. 4:17–24
[12] Genesis 5

one man's disobedience the many were made sinners."[13] Adam stood for all of us, acted for all of us, *rebelled* for all of us.

That reality often strikes people as being unfair. "I'd rather stand on my own," they say, "not be represented by another." Remarkably, though, it didn't seem to strike any of Adam's descendants that way. Probably that was at least partly because they knew that if God *had* let each and every one of them stand on their own, they wouldn't have done any better than Adam did. But it's also because they knew that their only hope of being saved was for God to send someone else—another representative, another *Adam*, so to speak—who would stand in their place again and this time save them. Adam had represented humanity in submission to Satan and rebellion against God; what was needed now was someone *else* to represent humanity in obedience to God and victory over Satan.

It All Came Down to This

And it turns out that's exactly what God promised to do.

Almost immediately, in the aftermath of Adam and Eve's sin, God promised that he would act to save humanity by sending another Representative, another Adam to stand in their place and, this time, win salvation for them. It's an amazing moment of hope when God makes that promise, because it comes at the darkest possible moment, when God is executing judgment against the Serpent who tempted Adam and Eve to sin in the first place. Here's how Genesis records what God said:

---

[13] Rom. 5:18–19

Because you have done this,

    cursed are you above all livestock

    and above all beasts of the field;

on your belly you shall go,

    and dust you shall eat

    all the days of your life.

I will put enmity between you and the woman,

    and between your offspring and her offspring;

he shall bruise your head,

    and you shall bruise his heel.[14]

Do you see the promise at the end? One day, God would send a Man to crush Satan's head once and for all. In other words, this Man would do what Adam *should* have done as humanity's representative, and in doing so, he would save them from the disaster their sin had brought on themselves and the entire world.

From that point forward, the promise of another Representative—another Adam—became humanity's great hope. Generation after generation looked forward to the day when God would make good on his promise, and from time to time they even wondered if *this* person or *that* person might be the promised Redeemer. So when Noah was born, his father Lamech exclaimed with hope, "Out of the ground that the LORD has cursed, this one shall bring us relief."[15] But of course it wasn't to be. Yes, like Adam, Noah became the representative of the human race, but almost immediately after he exited the

---

[14] Gen. 3:14–15
[15] Gen. 5:29

ark, he proved that he too was a sinner. This flawed second Adam failed just like the first, and it was clear that the great Redeemer had not yet come.

Throughout the ages, and ultimately through the history of Israel, the hopes of the people for the fulfillment of God's promises rested on one representative after another. Moses, Joshua, David, Solomon, the judges, the kings—each generation hoped that *this* might be the one. But each time, their hopes proved empty.

But then Jesus came, the last Adam who would stand as humanity's representative and do what the first Adam failed to do. That's why the confrontation between Jesus and Satan in the desert was so important. Not only was Jesus standing as Israel's Champion—the Davidic King—but he was also standing as humanity's Champion, the one who would win where humans' first father Adam had lost.

Do you remember the three temptations Satan used against Jesus in the wilderness? They were the three famous failings of Israel, yes, but they were also right at the heart of what Satan had tempted Adam and Eve to do in the garden. It's not hard to hear the echoes:

> Turn the stones into bread, Jesus; you're hungry; gratify yourself *now*.
> *Look at that fruit, Adam; it's pleasing to the eye; take it* now.
>
> Does God really keep his promises, Jesus? Well, I say he doesn't. Why don't you make him prove it?

Did God really say you'll die, Adam? Well, I say you won't. Let's put him to the test and see.

Bow down and worship me, Jesus, and I'll give you all the kingdoms of the world.
Obey me, Adam. Worship me, and I'll make you like God!

Jesus's battle against Satan that day was not just a personal one. Yes, he was experiencing temptation in order to be able to sympathize with his people, but he also was doing something that his people were never able to do—resist temptation all the way to the end of its strength, exhausting it, defeating it. And in the process, as he fought the battle on his people's behalf against their mortal enemy, he was doing what they should have done right from the start. He was honoring, obeying, and worshiping God *for them*, as their King and Representative and Champion.

But it wasn't over yet. Though Satan was defeated, the curse—"you shall surely die"—still hung over humanity's head like a sword. So even though King Jesus had defeated Satan, enduring his temptations to the end and in fact living an *entire life* of perfect righteousness before God, justice was still crying out that the sin of his people could not simply be ignored or set aside. They had rebelled against God, every one of them, and justice demanded nothing less than that the sentence God pronounced against them—spiritual death, separation from God, even divine wrath—be executed to the full. Anything less would have called God's very character into question.

You see, if King Jesus was going to save his people from their sins, it simply wasn't enough to defeat their great Enemy. After all, Satan had only *tempted* them to sin; they had made the choice themselves to rebel against God. That meant that the sentence of death was deserved, and it was still outstanding. In order to save his people, therefore, Jesus would have to exhaust that curse. He would have to let God's sentence of death—his righteous wrath against sinners—fall on him, instead of them. He would have to stand as their Substitute not only in life, but also in death.

It all came down to this: if his people were going to live, the Champion would have to die.

7

Lamb of God, Sacrifice for Man

John the Baptizer knew why Jesus had come, and he knew what Jesus would have to do in order to save his people.

Seeing Jesus walk down toward the Jordan River to be baptized, John pointed at him and cried out something that would have thrilled and confused the crowd all at the same time: "Behold, the Lamb of God, who takes away the sin of the world!"[1] The idea of a lamb being given to God in order to take away sin was intimately familiar to the Jews. But then again, why was John using that term to refer to a *person*? That was ominous. After all, everyone knew what happened to a lamb once it was given over to God as a sacrifice for sin.

Its throat was cut, and it bled to death.

Someone Had to Die

The Jewish sacrificial system is sometimes said to have its origin in Israel's escape from slavery in Egypt, but its deepest roots actually lie all the way back in the garden of Eden, in the

---

[1] John 1:29

sentence of death God pronounced over Adam and Eve when they chose to rebel against him. If you're going to understand the Jewish sacrifices—and ultimately the meaning of Jesus himself—you have to understand that when God said Adam and Eve would die if they sinned, he wasn't making an arbitrary decision. It's not as if he could have said, "In the day that you eat of it, you shall surely turn into a toad" or something.

The reason God declared *death* to be the consequence for sin is that it was perfectly fitting and right for him to do so. As Paul would put it later on in the New Testament, "The wages [that is, the earned and correct payment] of sin is death."[2] It's not hard to see why. First of all, when Adam and Eve sinned, they weren't breaking some unimportant rule that God had put in place. As we've already seen, they were choosing to try to throw off his authority over them. Essentially, they were declaring their independence from their God. Of course, the trouble was that it was that very God—the One from whom they were declaring their independence—who was the Source and Sustainer of their lives. He's the One who had breathed the breath of life into their lungs and who held them in existence, so when their relationship with him was broken—that is, when they were separated and cut off from him—their connection to the one and only Source of life was broken, too.

Not only that, but it is also right and good that God should be wrathful toward rebels. The Bible tells us that God is perfectly good and righteous and just in his very character. Given

---

[2] Rom. 6:23

that, it shouldn't be surprising that he reacts with hatred toward sin, which is by its very nature an embrace of evil and a rejection of what is good and right and just. Of course, God's wrath is not like ours; it's not explosive and out of control. It's exactly the opposite—an intense, settled opposition to sin and a commitment to destroy it. That's why God told Adam and Eve that they would die when they sinned, and it's why every human being now lives under that sentence of death: by our sin—by our exchange of the goodness of God for selfish evil—we have earned God's wrath and cut ourselves off from the Source of all life.

That's the deepest origin of Israel's sacrificial system. God was teaching his people that sin, by its very nature, deserves and demands death as its payment. But there was another principle God was teaching his people through the sacrifices, too, one that gave hope in the midst of what looked like abject hopelessness: *the penalty of death did not have to be paid by the sinner!*

Oh, it had to be paid by *someone*—death was still demanded for sin—but God, in love and mercy, allowed for the sentence of death to be executed on a substitute who would stand in the place of the sinner. If you think about it, you can see how this arrangement beautifully expressed both God's unbending justice *and* his mercy. The penalty demanded by sin would be paid, and justice would be satisfied, but the sinner himself would not necessarily die.

Maybe the most poignant example of this principle was the Festival of the Passover, the celebration of how God had finally rescued his people from their slavery in Egypt. The Passover festival looked back to one particular night when God dramatically and terribly executed the sentence of death on the people of Egypt. Over and over again through the prior few weeks, God had warned Pharaoh that his refusal to let the Israelites go was earning nothing but death for him and his people. And nine different times, God had dramatized his power and sovereignty over Egypt through a series of plagues that afflicted the nation. Through those plagues, God was confronting and defeating the gods of Egypt, driving them one at a time to their knees and proving to the Egyptians that he and he alone is God.

The horror of the plagues came to its crowning moment in the tenth one. Here is how God described to Moses what he was about to do to the people of Egypt:

> The LORD said to Moses, "Yet one plague more I will bring upon Pharaoh and upon Egypt. Afterward he will let you go from here. . . . About midnight I will go out in the midst of Egypt, and every firstborn in the land of Egypt shall die, from the firstborn of Pharaoh who sits on his throne, even to the firstborn of the slave girl who is behind the handmill, and all the firstborn of the cattle. There shall be a great cry throughout all the land of Egypt, such as there has never been, nor ever will be again. But not a dog shall growl against any of the people of Israel, either man or beast, that you may know that the LORD makes a distinction between Egypt and Israel."[3]

---

[3] Ex. 11:1, 4–7

This was a devastating judgment that God was about to pour out, but he also promised that his own people would be spared—*if* they would obey him and follow his instructions.

What God told his people to do must have been plenty frightening in itself. He told them that on the night the first-born were to die, each family was to take a lamb—not a defective one, but one without any flaw or blemish whatsoever—and kill it at twilight. Then the family was to make a feast of the animal. But even more importantly, God told them they must take some of the animal's blood and put it on the doorposts of their house. That was the key to it all, because God said that when he passed through the land of Egypt to kill the firstborn, he would see the blood on the doorposts and "pass over" that house, and the plague would not strike them. If they did all these things—if the lamb died and the family hid behind its blood—they would be saved.[4]

Now, stop and think for a second: you really have to wonder if the people of Israel were a little astonished to hear that God was going to go through *their* homes and villages, too! It hadn't happened that way for any of the previous nine plagues. In those, the frogs and the gnats and the flies and the locusts and the hail and the darkness and the blood and the boils had affected all of Egypt—except the towns where the Israelites had been settled. Up to this point, God had been careful to make a sharp separation between them and the Egyptians, and they hadn't had to do a thing except watch it all happen. But now, God tells them that he will visit their homes with the

---

[4] Ex. 12:1–13

plague of death, and they will die just like the Egyptians if they don't believe God and obey him.

The night when God went through the cities of Egypt, killing the firstborn one by one in judgment for the people's sin, would have been terrifying. The land would have filled with the screams of the Egyptians as their children died in the night. One wonders if they were joined by the screams and wails of regret from Israelites, too—the ones who had not believed and who had scoffed at God's word. The Bible simply doesn't say.

Do you see what God was teaching his people that night? For one thing, it was a shocking reminder of their own guilt. When all was said and done, God was reminding them that they were no less deserving of the judgment of death than the Egyptians. They themselves were guilty of sin.

But there was another lesson, too. Seared into their minds and hearts would have been the power and meaning of the substitutionary sacrifice. Killing the lamb was not a clean affair; it was visceral and bloody. The father would kneel down beside the animal, draw a knife, and slit the animal's throat, and the blood would spurt all over the ground until the animal staggered and gagged and fell into death. And as it happened, every eye would have instinctively risen from the dying lamb to one little boy, and the whole family would know: This lamb is dying so that little Joshua here won't. The lamb is dying in Joshua's place.

You see? God was teaching his people in a searing, visceral way that he wouldn't—indeed *couldn't*—simply sweep their sin away. Blood had to be shed because of it. Someone had to die, because that is the penalty that sin demands. And so as the father put the blood on the doorpost, scooped little Joshua into his arms, and shut the door of the house behind them, the whole family was learning that they were guilty and deserving of death. God wouldn't spare them because of their own innocence. He wouldn't save them because they were somehow less deserving of death than the Egyptians. No, he would pass over them because another had died in their place. As God passed over, with the drawn sword of judgment in his hand, they trusted in the blood of the lamb.

Not Just an Animal This Time

As time passed, God instituted a whole system of animal sacrifices whereby his people learned that their sin—real and evil as it was—could be borne and paid for by a substitute. But he also began to teach them that it would not always be animals who would bear the punishment for their sin.

One of the most significant examples of this is actually easy to miss, because it is so subtle. And yet it makes one of the most profound and important points in all the Old Testament. After they escaped from Egypt, the Israelites spent a good amount of time wandering around in the desert and—believe it or not—complaining that God was not giving them enough (or even *good* enough) food and water. Time and again, God provided for them, and time and again they complained and grumbled against him. In Exodus 17, the Bible tells us of an occasion that, at least at first glance, looks like just another time when Israel complained and God provided water. But actually, it was something infinitely more. God was about to teach his people something spectacular and wholly unexpected.

On this particular day, the people had come to a place called Rephidim, and as they had done so many times before, they began complaining that God had led them into the desert to kill them—this time by thirst. But here at Rephidim, the Israelites' complaining rose to new heights. This time, the Bible makes it clear that they were actually putting God on trial! Yes, it was Moses whom they were about to execute by stoning, but Moses was the spokesman for God. The people's real problem was not with Moses; it was with God. He had led them into the wilderness to die, and now they were charging him with murder!

The Bible describes God's instructions to Moses in the face of the people's charges against him. He tells Moses to gather the people together and stand before them with all the elders of Israel. Now that's significant because the elders were the ones who served as the nation's judges; they ruled in cases where charges like this were brought. Moreover, God tells Moses to bring his staff. That's a significant detail, too, because this wasn't just any staff. It was the staff with which Moses struck the Nile to turn to it to blood and the sand to turn it to gnats, and the one he held out over the Red Sea to make it crash down on the Egyptian army. In other words, it was a staff that Moses used for *judgment*.

The whole scene therefore cut a distinctly ominous form. The people were gathered, the elders were assembled, and the staff of judgment had been brought. It was as if God were saying to his rebellious, grumbling people, "You want to have a trial? OK, let's have a trial!" Someone was about to be condemned. Judgment was about to be meted out.

But against whom? Not against God, but against *Israel* for their complaining, for their grumbling, for their unfaithfulness to God when time after time after time God had been faithful to them. The staff of judgment was about to fall on *them*.

But then there's an amazing turn of events, really so subtle that even many long-time Christians don't see it. Look how the Bible describes what happened:

> So Moses cried to the LORD, "What shall I do with this people? They are almost ready to stone me." And the LORD said to Moses, "Pass on before the people, taking with you some of the elders of Israel, and take in your hand the staff with which you struck the Nile, and go. Behold, I will stand before you there on the rock at Horeb, and you shall strike the rock, and water shall come out of it, and the people will drink." And Moses did so, in the sight of the elders of Israel.[5]

Do you see it there, right in the middle of the paragraph? Do you see where the staff of judgment falls? On the rock, yes, but who is on the rock? *God is.* "I will stand before you there on the rock," God says, "and you shall strike it." In other words, "With the rod of judgment which by rights *should* fall on my people for their grumbling and sin and unfaithfulness," God insists, "you shall strike *me*." So Moses did, and what was the result? Life was unleashed; water flowed forth from the rock!

---

[5]Ex. 17:4–6

This was the great principle of substitution taken to a whole new level. Now it was not just an animal, but *God himself* taking the judgment and curse which should have fallen on his people! And because of that, they would live and not die.

Great King and Suffering Servant

Over the centuries, God taught his people more and more about the principle of substitution until the prophet Isaiah, more than anyone else in the Old Testament, finally tied it all together. We've already seen how Isaiah prophesied that a divine King would come to rule the world with perfect justice and righteousness, and to save God's people from their oppressors.[6] That would have been glorious enough in itself, but Isaiah also prophesied that this divine King—the one called "Mighty God"—would also fill the role of a Suffering Servant of God who would bear his people's sins in their place, taking the sentence of death they deserved.

Here's how Isaiah describes the work of this divine, royal Suffering Servant:

> Surely he has borne our griefs
>   and carried our sorrows;
> yet we esteemed him stricken,
>   smitten by God, and afflicted.
> But he was pierced for our transgressions;
>   he was crushed for our iniquities;
> upon him was the chastisement that brought us peace,

---

[6] Isa. 9:6–7

and with his wounds we are healed.
All we like sheep have gone astray;
    we have turned—every one—to his own way;
and the LORD has laid on him
    the iniquity of us all. . . .
Out of the anguish of his soul he shall see and be
        satisfied;
by his knowledge shall the righteous one, my servant,
    make many to be accounted righteous,
    and he shall bear their iniquities.[7]

Can you see what Isaiah is saying here? He's saying that this great King would not just establish a kingdom of perfect righteousness. As Suffering Servant, he would also take on himself—and exhaust!—the penalty of death for his people. He would absorb the curse that stood against them, and qualify them to live with him forever in the kingdom he had established.

He Knew Why He Had Come

All this is what John the Baptizer had in mind when he cried out that day, "Behold, the Lamb of God who takes away the sin of the world!"[8] He recognized Jesus to be the ultimate sacrifice who would die in his people's place, the long-foretold Suffering Servant who would be crushed for his people's iniquities.

And so, as we've seen, Jesus was baptized not because he needed to repent of his own sins, but because he was identifying

---

[7] Isa. 53:4–6, 11
[8] John 1:29

with and uniting himself to the sinful people he had come to save—as Son of God, as Representative, as King, as Champion, and as Suffering Servant of the Lord. That's the last piece of what the voice from heaven meant when it said, "This is my beloved Son, with whom I am well pleased."[9] Those words, "with whom I am well pleased," are a deliberate echo of words from the book of Isaiah that God first spoke about the Suffering Servant.

I hope you can see now the extraordinary thing that was happening that day on the banks of the Jordan River. With his baptism and these words from heaven, Jesus was stepping fully into the roles—the offices—that God intended him to fill from the very beginning. You might even say that with these words from heaven, God declares Jesus to be triply crowned—with the crown of heaven as God's Son, the crown of Israel as the long-awaited King, and the crown of thorns as the Suffering Servant who would save his people by dying for them, in their place.

It's not as if any of this was a surprise to Jesus. He knew why he had come, and he knew exactly what would be required of him to save his people from their sins. He would have to bear the wrath of God for his people. That's what he meant when he said that he had come to "give his life as a ransom for many."[10] It's what he meant when he handed his disciples a cup of wine at their last meal together before his death, and said, "Drink of it, all of you, for this is my blood of the covenant,

---

[9] Matt. 3:17
[10] Matt. 20:28

which is poured out for many for the forgiveness of sins."[11] The language was symbolic, but the reality behind it was earth-splittingly powerful. Jesus was about to die. The eternal Son of God, the long-awaited King, had already taken up the fallen sword and won his people's battle; now he was about to pay the penalty for their sin. The Suffering Servant was about to bear his people's iniquities, die in their place, and make them righteous before God.

No Other Way

The night before he died, Jesus shared one last supper with his disciples, and it proved to be one of his clearest explanations of what this all meant. Every year, the Jews celebrated the Passover by sharing a meal with one another. This meal was to remind them of the great deliverance God had accomplished when he saved them from slavery in Egypt. When Jesus and his disciples shared this supper, therefore, they were celebrating an amazing salvation. But Jesus had other intentions. As he shared this supper with them, he explained that now an even greater act of salvation was about to take place, one that would rescue God's people not just from physical slavery and death, but from *spiritual* slavery and death. An act of love even greater than the exodus was about to be performed. Here's what Jesus said at the Last Supper:

> Now as they were eating, Jesus took bread, and after blessing it broke it and gave it to the disciples, and said,

---

[11] Matt. 26:27–28

"Take, eat; this is my body." And he took a cup, and when he had given thanks he gave it to them, saying, "Drink of it, all of you, for this is my blood of the covenant, which is poured out for many for the forgiveness of sins.[12]

This is where Jesus's love for his disciples had brought him: his blood would be spilled so that they could be saved. He would die so that they could be freed and forgiven of their sin, their faithlessness, and their rebellion against God.

What comes next is one of those places in Scripture where you almost fear to tread. It's just too intimate, and too agonizing. After dinner, Jesus takes his disciples to a garden called Gethsemane. He knows what's coming, so he goes away to pray. The prayer Jesus prays, there in the garden, is agonizing, but it shows us again the love that led Jesus to endure the cross: "He fell on his face and prayed, saying, 'My Father, if it be possible, let this cup pass from me; nevertheless, not as I will, but as you will.'"[13]

You see, there was in fact a way for the cup—the cup of God's wrath, which Jesus was about to drink—to pass. There was a way for him *not* to have to drink it at all—and that way was to let us sinners be condemned and sentenced to death forever. That's what Jesus meant when he said that he had twelve legions of angels at his disposal. Seventy-two thousand angels stood ready, at a moment's notice, at a *whisper* from his lips, to bring Jesus back to heaven in glory, to the praise and worship of billions upon billions of angels who would have

---

[12] Matt. 26:26–28
[13] Matt. 26:39

honored him forever as the perfectly just, perfectly righteous Son of God.

But he didn't call them. He let them stand on the edge of heaven, wondering at the whole scene, because he and his Father were determined to save their fallen people. And once that determination was made, there was only one way to do it—Jesus would have to drink the cup of God's wrath. That was Jesus's question there in the garden: "Is there another way to save them, Father? Can these people possibly be saved in another way than by my bearing the penalty of death and separation from you?" And the answer came back, silent but unmistakable: "No. There is no other way."

Why? Because God couldn't sweep sin under the rug. He couldn't ignore it, or pretend it hadn't happened, or forgive it outright. He would have to *deal* with it—really, justly, righteously. After all, as the psalmist said, "Righteousness and justice are the foundation of your throne."[14] That's why Jesus would drink the cup of God's wrath—because he loved us and wanted to save us, yes, but also because he loved God the Father and would not see his glory diminished in the process. We would be saved, and God would be glorified.

But only if Jesus the King died.

As He Hung There Dying

The Roman practice of crucifixion will remain as one of the most gruesome, humiliating, and altogether obscene methods of execution the world has ever known. So horrible was it, in

---

[14] Ps. 89:14; 97:2

fact, that the sophisticated and cultured people in Greek and Roman societies would not even utter the word *cross* in polite company. That was a reviled word, and it referred to an even more reviled and hated form of death.

Crucifixion in the Roman world was never a private event. It was always raw, open, and searingly public. That's because its entire purpose was to terrify the masses into submission to the authorities. The Romans made sure that crosses holding the broken, writhing bodies of the dying—or the rotting corpses of the dead—frequently lined the main roads into cities. They even scheduled mass public crucifixions to coincide with civic and religious festivals in order to ensure that the maximum number of people would witness the horror. Murderers, robbers, traitors, and especially slaves were crucified—brutally— by the thousands, all over the empire and always in full public view. The horror of the cross was inescapable in Roman life, and the Roman authorities intended it to be that way.

Given the number and frequency of crosses in Roman society, it's somewhat surprising that ancient accounts of crucifixion are so rare. But then again, nobody wanted much to write about such a thing. And why would they? The cross was a government-sanctioned—even government *encouraged*—opportunity for executioners to carry out on condemned people their most sadistic, brutal, and viciously inventive fantasies. So, perhaps not surprisingly at all, the accounts we have of it are generally short, and the authors usually only allude to the horrors rather than describe them in any detail. "You wouldn't want to know," they seem to say.

Shredded flesh against unforgiving wood, iron stakes pounded through bone and wracked nerves, joints wrenched out of socket by the sheer dead weight of the body, public humiliation before the eyes of family, friends, and the world— that was death on the cross, "the infamous stake" as the Romans called it, "the barren wood," the *maxima mala crux*. Or as the Greeks spat it out, the *stauros*. Really, it's no wonder no one talked about it. It's no wonder parents hid their children's eyes from it. The *stauros* was a loathsome thing, and the one who died on it was loathsome too, a vile criminal whose only use was to hang there as a putrid, decaying warning to anyone else who might follow his example.

That is how Jesus died.

This crucifixion, though, was unlike any that anyone had ever seen. Everything about it said that the man hanging on *this* cross was not ordinary. Something unusual was happening here.

For one thing, there was the way Jesus *acted* while he hung on the cross—what he said to those around him. Most of the criminals who were crucified on Roman crosses spent their last hours either begging for mercy, hurling insults at the soldiers and people watching them, or simply groaning in pain. Not Jesus. Even as he hung there, enduring the insults of the Jewish rulers, the taunts of the men crucified alongside him, and the cold, calculating disinterest of the Roman soldiers, he seemed to be moved by love for those who were killing him. When one of the men crucified alongside him seemed to recognize him for who he was, Jesus told him, "Truly, I say to you, today you will be with me in Paradise."[15] As the soldiers threw dice at the foot of the cross to divide up his clothing, he looked to heaven and prayed, "Father, forgive them, for they know not what they do."[16] Amazingly, even as he hung there dying, Jesus was loving and saving and giving hope to those around him.

There was also his endurance of the mockery—the *unending* mockery. The Romans had started it during the flogging, dressing Jesus in a strip of purple fabric, putting a reed in his hand to serve as a scepter, and shaping a bundle of thorns into a crown and pressing it down on his head. Then they bowed down to him in laughter and cried out, "Hail, King of the Jews!" It was meant as much to humiliate the entire nation of the Jews as to mock Jesus, and yet as he hung on the cross, Jesus's own people joined in ridiculing him. "If you are the Son of God," one said, "come down from the cross!" Another said: "He saved others; he cannot save himself." Through all that, Jesus said nothing in return. Though he knew that so much of what they said was ironically *true*, he simply endured.[17]

Then there was the darkness. The Gospel writers tell us that from the sixth hour until the ninth hour—that is, from about noon until three o'clock in the afternoon—a thick darkness covered Jerusalem. Much ink has been spilled through history trying to explain what that darkness was: perhaps an eclipse, or a dust storm, or even volcanic activity. But the people who

---

[15] Luke 23:43
[16] Luke 23:34
[17] Matt. 27:29, 40, 42

saw it happen understood it to be an act of God himself. Luke simply says that "the sun's light failed."[18]

In fact, the darkness that covered the land that day was deeply symbolic of what was happening on the cross as Jesus died. You see, over and over again in the Bible, *darkness* is how the judgment of God is described. It's the blackness of death and the grave. There on Golgotha, that darkness of judgment enveloped Jesus, the Son of God, the Suffering Servant.

When it lifted, Matthew tells us that Jesus cried out in a loud voice, "Eli, Eli, lema sabachthani?" which is Aramaic for, "My God, my God, why have you forsaken me?"[19] It was a quotation from Psalm 22, a song in which King David symbolically suffers in the place of Israel. But what did Jesus mean by it? He meant that in that moment, under the darkness of judgment, he was representing his people by taking in his own soul the punishment they deserved—to be abandoned and shut out and cast off and banished and forsaken by God. You see, as he hung there on the cross, all the sin of God's people was placed on Jesus, and he died for them. In their place. As their Champion. Their Substitute. Their King.

Thus the ancient sentence of death first pronounced in Eden was executed. The curse was inflicted. Jesus the Son of God was forsaken by his Father because of his people's sins, and with a loud cry of "It is finished," he died.[20]

What happened next is nothing short of beautiful. Matthew tells us that the curtain of the temple—the sixty-foot-high

---

[18] Luke 23:45
[19] Matt. 27:46
[20] John 19:30

woven screen that separated the people from the Most Holy Place where God's presence dwelt—was torn in two from top to bottom.[21] With that, God signaled to humanity that their long exile from his presence was finally and forever over. After so many millennia, since the day Adam and Eve first looked back with tears after being exiled from Eden, humans were welcome once again to enter into the Most Holy Place, and come into the presence of God.

The Suffering Servant, the King of kings, the Champion of humanity had finished his work. By his life, he had done everything righteousness demanded. By his blood, he had paid the penalty his people deserved for their sin. He had reversed Satan's triumph. He had won salvation, once and for all!

And now, he was dead.

---

[21] Matt. 27:51

8

Resurrected and Reigning Lord

The two criminals crucified with Jesus were still alive, and it was getting late in the day on Friday. In any other city, the Romans probably would have let them hang there on the crosses through the night, maybe even giving them bits of food and water so they'd stay alive and suffer for days. They decided not to do that this time, though, not in Jerusalem. Though the Romans kept any conquered people firmly under heel, they were usually relatively respectful of the religious traditions of those they dominated. So it was with the Jews, and the Romans agreed to respect their weekly day of rest, the Sabbath, which ran from sundown on Friday until sundown on Saturday. So when the Jewish rulers asked the governor to do something to make sure the bodies wouldn't remain on the crosses through the Sabbath, the governor agreed.

That meant these three crucified men would need to die quickly, so the order was given for the soldiers to perform what they called *crurifragium*. In a way, it was a cold mercy when a soldier walked up to one of the men nailed up beside Jesus, swung the staff of his spear at his legs, and splintered his shins. The man would have screamed, but the agony would be over more quickly now. Because he couldn't push himself up to breathe, the man would die within a few minutes. The same thing was done to the other man, but when they came to Jesus, spear in hand, the soldiers realized that he was already dead. That was something of a surprise to them; usually the crucified didn't die so quickly. So just to make sure, one of them raised his spear and thrust it deep into Jesus's side. When he pulled it out, a mixture of separated blood and water poured from the wound—an unmistakable, beyond-a-shadow-of-doubt sign of death.

Some of Jesus's followers, including his mother, were there at Golgotha watching all this. They saw the soldiers nail his wrists to the cross, then drive another iron stake through his feet. They watched as the cross was lifted into place; they saw the sun blink out at noon; they heard Jesus cry out in agony as he experienced the abandonment of God; they heard him cry out that his work was finished; they watched as he slumped forward and died. And now it fell to them to dispose of his body. The Romans wouldn't do it for them.

One of Jesus's followers, a wealthy man named Joseph of Arimathea, had kept his belief in Jesus quiet until now, but for whatever reason, he decided at this point to go public with it. So he went to the governor and asked if he might take charge of Jesus's body. Joseph had a tomb in a nearby garden that had just been cut, and he wanted to lay Jesus there. Pilate gave permission, and so Joseph and some of Jesus's other disciples began the unpleasant work of preparing his body for burial. The cross was lowered, the iron spikes were wrenched out of his wrists and ankles, and the crown of thorns they'd put on his head was tossed aside. Then the men began to embalm his body with spices and oils, seventy-five pounds of it, one writer tells us.[1]

The sun was setting, though, and they couldn't finish the job in time. They would have to come back early on Sunday morning, after the Sabbath had ended. For now, they simply wrapped Jesus's body in cloths, carried it to the tomb, and laid it inside. Then they rolled a large stone over the opening to seal it, and went home.

I've often wondered what that Saturday was like for those who had given their lives to following Jesus for the last three years. Probably the events of the past few days swirled in their minds, and they must have wondered what they'd been thinking. For all the promises, the miracles, the prophecies, the claims, it was all finished now. I'm sure they had questions—lots of them—but what they knew for sure was that Jesus was dead now, just like anyone else. The Romans had made a gruesome, public example of him, and the Jewish leaders had gotten rid of another problem. And their hopes—which they had put entirely in Jesus, the one they had hoped was the Christ, the Son of the Living God—had died with him.

So I wonder what that Saturday was like. The Bible tells us that the disciples scattered after Jesus was arrested, and it seems that they mostly went into hiding. As far as we know,

---

[1] John 19:38–42

only a small number were even present at the crucifixion. After all, they were right to worry that the authorities would soon come after the followers of this "false messiah" and kill them, too. So they cowered in their homes, or in friends' homes, hoping to escape Rome's wrath. And probably, they wept. What else do you do when everything you hoped for turns out to have been nothing but delusion, a wish that vanished into thin air?

Jesus, the "Son of God." The "Christ." The "King of Israel." The "Heir of David." The "Last Adam." The "Suffering Servant."

All that was a delusion.

Here was the stark reality:

Jesus was a carpenter.
From Nazareth.
He was their friend.
And now he was dead.

That's what Mary and the other women must have been feeling, too, on Sunday, when they went to Jesus's tomb. They weren't going that morning to see if Jesus had kept his brazen promise to rise from the dead. At that point, they didn't even remember he had said such things. No, they were going to finish the job of embalming his body, because they hadn't had time to do so before sunset on Friday. So now, at the first chance they had, they walked to a tomb to embalm a two-day-old, dead, crucified body.

That's what they expected—a gruesome, sad, and unpleasant morning. But it's not what they got.

In fact, what they saw when they arrived at the tomb shocked them, and it changed the history of the world. Here's how Mark tells it:

> When the Sabbath was past, Mary Magdalene, Mary the mother of James, and Salome bought spices, so that they might go and anoint him. And very early on the first day of the week, when the sun had risen, they went to the tomb. And they were saying to one another, "Who will roll away the stone for us from the entrance of the tomb?" And looking up, they saw that the stone had been rolled back—it was very large. And entering the tomb, they saw a young man sitting on the right side, dressed in a white robe, and they were alarmed. And he said to them, "Do not be alarmed. You seek Jesus of Nazareth, who was crucified. He has risen; he is not here. See the place where they laid him. But go, tell his disciples and Peter that he is going before you to Galilee. There you will see him, just as he told you."[2]

It took a while for the reality to set in. After all, they hadn't actually seen Jesus; they'd just been told by this "young man" in a white robe—an angel—that Jesus was alive. The women ran quickly to tell the disciples, and then they too came to the tomb, looked in, and saw Jesus's grave clothes neatly folded up and placed to the side. Then they went home, and marveled and wondered—and hoped.

A woman named Mary Magdalene, a long-time disciple,

---
[2] Mark 16:1–7

was the first person to see the resurrected Jesus. After the other disciples left the tomb, Mary stayed behind, weeping. Stooping to look again into the empty tomb, she was startled to see two angels now, sitting on the ledge where Jesus's body had lain. "Woman, why are you weeping?" they asked her. She answered them, "They have taken away my Lord, and I do not know where they have laid him."[3] Now, just pause for a second and take this in: even after all that had happened—the stone rolled away, the empty tomb, the angels telling them Jesus wasn't here among the dead—Jesus's closest followers were not quick to believe that he had come back to life. They were *miles away* from the gullible saps they've sometimes been made out to be. For crying out loud, Mary Magdalene even looks into the face of an angel and tells him that *her opinion* is that someone has moved his body!

At that moment, the writer John tells us, Jesus appeared behind her. She had no idea it was him, though, and just thought he was the gardener. "Woman," he asked, "why are you weeping?" So Mary told him: "Sir, if you have carried him away, tell me where you have laid him."[4] Perhaps the gardener had moved the body for some reason, she thought. Jesus didn't answer the question.

It was time for Mary to know.

So "Jesus said to her, 'Mary.'" Just her name, with all the love and compassion and power with which he had always said it. And then Mary knew. "She turned and said to him in Ara-

---

[3] John 20:13
[4] John 20:15

maic, 'Rabboni!' (which means Teacher)."[5] It was him! At the end of it all, here was Jesus the crucified, alive again!

Over the next forty days, Jesus came again and again to his disciples, sometimes in small groups, sometimes in very large ones. He spoke to them together, and he called some of them aside to speak to them individually. He taught them, he explained the significance of all that had happened, and he helped them believe that he really was *there*! When they wondered if he were a ghost, he ate some fish. When Peter was wracked by guilt for denying him, he forgave him. One of the disciples, Thomas, even flatly declared that he would never believe that Jesus had been resurrected, not unless he could put his finger in the nail holes and his hand into the spear wound in his side. Then about a week later, while they were all together and the doors were locked, Jesus came. It's not that he knocked on the door and walked in. No, the people who were there said he just . . . *came* . . . and there he was! Immediately Jesus turned to Thomas and offered his hand: "Put your finger here," he said, "and see my hands; and put out your hand, and place it in my side. Do not disbelieve, but believe." Thomas was thunderstruck. All in an instant, he knew, and he said to Jesus, "My Lord and my God!"[6]

You have to realize that the man who now stood before them wasn't just someone who had been *resuscitated*, as if he just hadn't been quite dead on the cross and had managed to claw his way back to life. He wasn't even someone who had just

---

[5] John 20:16
[6] John 20:27–28

been called back out of death, like the widow's son or Lazarus. No, with Jesus, it was more like he had gone *through* death and come out the other side. The wounds were still there, but they didn't need to be treated or healed. Now they stood as glorious proof of how death had taken him for a moment, and how he had conquered it. For the disciples, that meant that everything had changed. Despair had given way to triumph, death to life, condemnation to salvation, and abject defeat to astonishing victory.

Jesus was alive.

The Resurrection of Jesus:
Hinge, Foundation, and Capstone

The resurrection of Jesus has been massively controversial throughout the centuries, and the great question driving it all has always been, did it happen? The controversy is understandable, because the stakes are enormous. Think about it: if Jesus really did get up from the dead after having been crucified, then something breathtakingly extraordinary has happened, and we had all better listen to him because everything he ever claimed for himself—that he's the Son of God, the King of kings, the Lord of life, the Suffering Servant, the second person of the Trinity—has been vindicated. On the other hand, if he *didn't* rise from the dead, well then never mind. It's all over, it never should have become such a big deal in human history in the first place, and we can all go about our lives because Jesus was just one of a thousand first-century Jews who made grandiose claims about himself and then died. Full stop.

Do you see why Christians make such a big deal of this? The resurrection is the hinge on which all Christianity turns. It's the foundation on which everything else rests, the capstone that holds everything else about Christianity together. Which means—*crucially*—that when Christians assert that Jesus rose from the dead, they are making a *historical* claim, *not a religious one*. Yes of course there are "religious" implications to that claim, if you want to call them that, but none of those are in the least valid if Jesus didn't really, truly, historically come back to life from the dead. Even the early Christians understood this. They weren't interested in just creating a nice religious story that would encourage people, help them live better lives, and perhaps provide them with a metaphor of hope blooming out of despair that might help them endure the storms of this life. No, the early Christians wanted the world to know that they really believed that Jesus had *gotten up out of the grave*, and they themselves knew that if he didn't really do that, then everything they stood for was empty and false and utterly worthless. It's like Paul said in one of his letters: "If Christ has not been raised, then our preaching is in vain and your faith is in vain. . . . If Christ has not been raised, your faith is futile and you are still in your sins. . . . If in Christ we have hope in this life only, we are of all people most to be pitied."[7]

In other words, if Jesus didn't rise from the dead, Christians are pathetic people.

But here's the other side of that coin: if Jesus *did* rise from the dead, then every human being is confronted with a demand

---

[7] 1 Cor. 15:14–19

to believe what he said, to acknowledge him as King, and to submit to him as Savior and Lord. And of course, my friend, that includes *you*.

That's why it's so important for you—yes, you, right there reading this book—to come to a decision about what you think about the resurrection of Jesus. It's not enough to just withhold judgment on something like this. You need to give it some thought and decide either "Yes, I think this happened. I think Jesus rose from the dead, and I believe he is who he claimed to be," or, "No, I don't think it happened, and I reject his claims." Sometimes you hear people say that it's legitimate for them to have no opinion about the resurrection because one can't get to the truth or untruth of religious claims. But like we said before: Christians aren't making a *religious* claim when they say Jesus rose from the grave. They're making a *historical* one; they're saying that this thing happened just as surely and really as it happened that Julius Caesar became emperor of Rome. It's the kind of claim that can be thought about and investigated; it can be judged, and you can come to a conclusion about it.

Do you think it happened, or not?

Here's the fundamental truth about Christians: we *do* think it happened.

We don't think the disciples were experiencing some kind of mass hallucination. That doesn't even make sense given how many times people saw Jesus, over how much time, and in how many different groups.

We also don't think it was all a big mistake. The last thing the Jewish rulers wanted was a rumor of a resurrected messiah floating around, so the first thing they would have done in the face of such a rumor was produce the body to put a stop to it. They never did that. And on the other hand, if Jesus had somehow managed to survive his crucifixion, exactly how likely is it that this staggering, wounded, crucified, and spear-stabbed man would have been able to convince his stubborn, skeptical followers that he was the Lord of life and the Conqueror of death? Not highly likely, I'd say.

For that matter, we Christians also don't think the disciples were perpetrating a hoax or a plot. If they were, what exactly would they have been hoping to get out of it? And why didn't they pull the plug when it became clear they weren't going to get what they were after—perhaps, for instance, just before the Romans chopped their heads off or drove the nails through their own wrists?

No, it wasn't a hallucination, or a mistake, or a plot. Something else happened, and it was something that had the power to turn these cowardly, skeptical men into *martyrs* of Jesus, eyewitnesses who were willing to stake everything on him, and endure everything—even torturous death—for the sake of telling the world, "This man Jesus was crucified, but now he is *alive!*"

Authority to Rule and Judge—and Save

After that first Sunday, Jesus spent the next forty days teaching his disciples and commissioning them to proclaim his kingship to the world. Then, he ascended into heaven. Now that may sound to you like another load of mythological, religious language that doesn't really mean anything, but the biblical writers didn't see it that way at all. Actually, they describe Jesus's ascent into heaven in the most literal words imaginable:

> As they were looking on, he was lifted up, and a cloud took him out of their sight. And while they were gazing into heaven as he went, behold, two men stood by them in white robes, and said, "Men of Galilee, why do you stand looking into heaven? This Jesus, who was taken up from you into heaven, will come in the same way as you saw him go into heaven."[8]

It was the kind of thing that left the disciples with their necks craned up, looking into the clouds, wondering where Jesus had gone. It wasn't just a spiritual ascension; it was a physical one.

But more important than the *fact* of Jesus's ascension into heaven is its *significance*. See, it wasn't just a way for Jesus to conveniently disappear from the scene. It was God's act of enthroning him and investing him with final and full authority to rule and to judge—and, wonderfully, to save! If you know yourself to be a sinner who deserves God's wrath for your rebellion against him, then the fact that Jesus now sits on the throne of the universe is astonishingly good news. It means that the great King who will ultimately judge you and sentence you is also one who loves you and who invites you to take salvation and mercy and grace from his hand.

That's what the Bible means when it says, "Everyone who

---

[8] Acts 1:9–11

calls on the name of the Lord will be saved."[9] It means that Jesus, the resurrected and reigning King, the One to whom God has granted all authority in heaven and on earth, has the right and authority to save people from their sin.

What Do You Do Now?

Now, let me ask you a question. If all this really is true, then what's next for you? If Jesus really did rise from the dead, if he really is who he claimed to be, then what do you do now?

Let me tell you what Jesus said you should do. It's not difficult or complicated, and we know what it is because Jesus told us very clearly. Over and over as he was teaching people, loving them, confronting them in their sin, and telling them who he was and that he could save them, he told them that he wanted them to believe in him—in other words, to have *faith* in him. "Repent and *believe* the gospel," he said. "For God so loved the word," one biblical writer said, "that he gave his only Son, that whoever *believes* in him should not perish but have eternal life."[10]

Sadly, for most people today, the words *believe* and *faith* have been drained of meaning. For us they're sappy words, bound up with things like Santa Claus and the Easter Bunny and fairies and magic dragons. Centuries ago, though, *faith* and *belief* were powerful, serious words. They spoke to strength, reliability, faithfulness, and the trust given to someone who had proven himself worthy of it. That's the kind of thing Jesus

---

[9] Rom. 10:13
[10] Mark 1:15; John 3:16

was talking about when he told people to "believe" in him. He didn't mean that you should just come to the conclusion that he exists; he meant that you should *rely* on him. You should look at his claims, his words, and his actions, and decide if you think he is worthy of your trust, worthy of staking your life on him.

But what does that mean? What exactly are we trusting Jesus for? Well, the whole story of the Bible, as we've seen, teaches us that we are all rebels against God. We have sinned against him, broken his law, and thrown off his authority over our lives in a million different ways, and because of that sin, we deserve to suffer the penalty that sin has always rightly brought—death. We deserve to die physically, yes, but even worse we deserve to have God pour out his infinite wrath on us. Death—that's the wages our sin has earned for us.

Therefore what we need, more than anything else in the world, is to be declared righteous before God, instead of guilty. We need him to hand down a verdict on us that is in our favor rather than against us. And this is where faith in Jesus comes in. Here is the good news, the gospel, of Jesus Christ: the whole reason Jesus came was so that he could stand in the place of sinners like you and me, doing what we ought to have done from the very beginning, and exhausting the death-curse that stands against us. To have faith in Jesus, therefore, is a massively significant act. When we believe in Jesus, trust in him, and rely on him, the Bible says that we are united to him as our King and Representative and Substitute. All of a sudden, therefore, our life's record of unrighteousness, disobedience, and rebellion against God is credited to Jesus, and he dies because of it, on our behalf and in our place. And at the same time, Jesus's perfect life of obedience and fellowship with God is credited to *us*, and on the basis of that perfect life, God declares us to be righteous.

You see? When you are united to Jesus by relying on him for salvation, a magnificent exchange takes place: Jesus gets your sin and dies for it. And you get Jesus's righteousness, and live because of it! But then there's so much more: being united to Jesus through faith means that everything that comes to Jesus *by right* because he perfectly obeyed the Father also becomes yours! None of the blessings of salvation is ours by right; we don't deserve any of them. But all of them are Jesus's by right, and we receive them because we are united to him in an embrace of desperate, trusting faith. So Jesus is declared to be righteous, and therefore *you* are declared to be righteous. He is glorified, and therefore *you* are glorified. He is raised from the dead, and therefore *you*—because you are united to him—are raised to spiritual life now with a promise of physical resurrection later. That's why the Bible calls Jesus "the firstfruits" of the resurrection.[11] He lives by right; we live by union with him.

That's not to say, of course, that Jesus stands as Representative and Substitute for everyone in the world. No, he stands as Substitute for those who acknowledge that he really is who he says he is, who recognize that he really can do what he says he can do, and who therefore put their faith, their trust, and their reliance in him. Look, we all as human beings are in open

---

[11] 1 Cor. 15:20

rebellion against the God who made us. Because of that, God was under no obligation at all to do anything to save us. In fact, he could have simply destroyed us and sent us all to hell, and the angels of heaven would have praised him for all eternity for his unimpeachable justice. "Thus always to rebels against the Most High God!" they would have said. But God, simply and solely because he loved us, sent his Son Jesus to offer mercy to all of us rebels who would come and bow their knee to him, and acknowledge him and embrace him as our rightful King. And when we do, he also—with incredible love—agrees to stand as our Substitute, crediting his righteous life to our account and taking on himself the penalty of death that stands against us.

That's also not to say that faith in Jesus is without reper-cussions in your life. No, when you put faith in Jesus, you're acknowledging him as your Substitute and Representative. In other words, you're recognizing him as your King, and that means he will begin to exercise authority in your life, calling you to turn away from your sin and rebellion against God. That turning away from sin is what the Bible calls *repentance*. It means that you declare war against sin and strive to grow in righteousness so that you look more and more like Jesus. It's not as if you do that alone, though. When you're united to Jesus by faith, the Bible says that the Holy Spirit—the third person of the Trinity—comes to live in you, and it is he who gives you power and desire to fight sin and strive toward righteousness.

So that's it! That's what it means to have faith in Jesus. It means that you rely on him to save you when there's no way you'll be able to save yourself. It means that you recognize that you have no hope on your own of standing before God and enduring the sentence of death that rightly stands against you, much less of earning a righteous verdict when he looks at your life's record. But then it also means that you believe that Jesus *has already* exhausted that death sentence on behalf of sinners just like you, that he *has already* earned the righteous verdict that you need, and that your only hope is to rely on him—100 percent—to stand in your place as your Substitute.

That's what King Jesus—risen from the dead and reigning from heaven—invites every human being to do. It's an open invitation, with no restrictions, no strings, no fine print. King Jesus's hand will not always be outstretched and open, but for now, it is. The only question is whether you will take it, fall on your knees before him in acknowledgment, and trust him to stand in your place under God's judgment—or whether you will decide to stand under that judgment on your own.

The choice is yours. At least for a little while.

A Final Word

Who Do You Say He Is?

At least for a little while.

That wasn't just rhetorical. The fact is, King Jesus's hand will not be extended in mercy forever. One day, perhaps even one day soon, the day of mercy will be over and the day of judgment will arrive. Jesus promised, as his death on the cross loomed ever nearer, that he would one day return to judge human beings once and for all. The day of salvation and mercy and grace is only so long, and that means that one day, the choice will no longer be yours. It will be made for you, and the choice that will be made is that you will be cast away from God, from Jesus, forever.

That's why it's so important for you to come to some answer to the question, who is Jesus? *now*. I hope that in reading this book, you've realized that if nothing else, that isn't a question that can be nicely ignored. Whatever you wind up thinking about Jesus, the fact remains that he makes strong, even invasive claims about you and your relationship to God. Sure, you can ignore those claims—you can ignore anything if you try hard enough—but when somebody says, "You are a rebel against the God who made you, and his sentence against you is death. But I have come to stand in your place, to take that penalty, and to save you," that's something you probably should pay attention to.

Maybe you're not ready yet to put your faith in Jesus. If so, why not? What other questions do you have? What is holding you back? Once you identify those things, don't just walk away from them. Examine them. Pursue them. Find answers to your questions. This issue—"Who Is Jesus?"—is of crucial importance. Don't ignore it or put it off. If you come to the conclusion that "no, I don't believe that Jesus is who the Bible says he is; I don't believe he is who he claimed to be," then so be it. At least there's some solidity there.

But, my friend, here's my plea: don't be caught at the moment of judgment saying, "I should have thought it through; I should have pursued it; I should have taken the time to come up with an answer!" Every other regret, on the last day, will pale in comparison with that.

On the other hand, maybe you're ready to say, "Yeah, I really do think Jesus is the King, the Son of God, the Suffering Servant. I know I'm a sinner and a rebel against God, and I know I deserve death for that rebellion, and I know Jesus can save me." If so, then you need to know that becoming a Christian is not a difficult thing. There are no rites to perform, no specific words to say, no deeds to perform. You simply turn away from sin and trust Jesus, lean on him, and rely on him to save you.

And then you tell the world! *This* is who Jesus is. He is the One who saves people just like me.

And just
like
you!

About the Series

The 9Marks series of books is premised on two basic ideas. First, the local church is far more important to the Christian life than many Christians today perhaps realize. We at 9Marks believe that a healthy Christian is a healthy church member.

Second, local churches grow in life and vitality as they organize their lives around God's Word. God speaks. Churches should listen and follow. It's that simple. When a church listens and follows, it begins to look like the One it is following. It reflects his love and holiness. It displays his glory. A church will look like him as it listens to him. By this token, the reader might notice that all "9 marks," taken from Mark Dever's book, *Nine Marks of a Healthy Church* (Crossway, 3rd ed., 2013), begin with the Bible:

- expositional preaching;
- biblical theology;
- a biblical understanding of the gospel;
- a biblical understanding of conversion;
- a biblical understanding of evangelism;
- a biblical understanding of church membership;
- a biblical understanding of church discipline;

- a biblical understanding of discipleship and growth; and
- a biblical understanding of church leadership.

More can be said about what churches should do in order to be healthy, such as pray. But these nine practices are the ones that we believe are most often overlooked today (unlike prayer). So our basic message to churches is, don't look to the best business practices or the latest styles; look to God. Start by listening to God's Word again.

Out of this overall project comes the 9Marks series of books. These volumes intend to examine the nine marks more closely and from different angles. Some target pastors. Some target church members. Hopefully all will combine careful biblical examination, theological reflection, cultural consideration, corporate application, and even a bit of individual exhortation. The best Christian books are always both theological and practical.

It's our prayer that God will use this volume and the others to help prepare his bride, the church, with radiance and splendor for the day of his coming.

IX 9Marks

Building Healthy Churches

9Marks exists to equip church leaders with a biblical vision and practical resources for displaying God's glory to the nations through healthy churches.

To that end, we want to see churches characterized by these nine marks of health:

1   Expositional Preaching
2   Biblical Theology
3   A Biblical Understanding of the Gospel
4   A Biblical Understanding of Conversion
5   A Biblical Understanding of Evangelism
6   Biblical Church Membership
7   Biblical Church Discipline
8   Biblical Discipleship
9   Biblical Church Leadership

Find all our Crossway titles
and other resources at
www.9Marks.org

Other 9Marks Books

Building Healthy Churches

Edited by Mark Dever and Jonathan Leeman

Download a

free study guide

for *Who is Jesus?*

crossway.org/WhoIsJesus

Also Available from Greg Gilbert

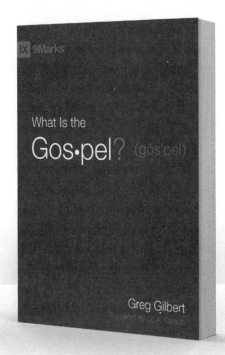

"Greg Gilbert, with a sharp mind and a pastor's heart, has written a book that will be helpful for seekers, new Christians, and anyone who wants to understand the gospel with greater clarity. I've been waiting for a book like this!"

KEVIN DEYOUNG, Senior Pastor, University Reformed Church, East Lansing, Michigan

"This little book on the gospel is one of the clearest and most important books I've read in recent years."

MARK DEVER, Senior Pastor, Capitol Hill Baptist Church, Washington DC